**David Cooper** is a specialist in the assessment and development of senior executives and supports investors in managing leadership risk. For the first eleven years of his career he worked in the risk advisory group at Arthur Andersen. He then completed a Masters degree in Organisational Psychology at the London School of Economics, where he began to develop the concept of 'leadership risk'. He went on to become one of the few Chartered Accountants to qualify as a Chartered Psychologist and founded Cooper Limon, a professional advisory business specialising in management due diligence and portfolio review for Private Equity and Strategic investors. Through Cooper Limon and in his role as head of executive assessment at Praesta Partners, an international coaching firm, he has assessed and coached several hundred senior executives and advised some of the world's leading Private Equity funds. He continues his research into leadership risk and has spoken internationally at both Accounting and Psychology conferences.

Leadership Risk

Leadership Risk

*A Guide for Private Equity
and Strategic Investors*

David Cooper

A John Wiley and Sons, Ltd., Publication

Library of Congress Cataloging-in-Publication Data

Cooper, David.
  Leadership risk : a guide for private equity and strategic investors / David Cooper.
    p. cm.
  ISBN 978-0-470-03264-0
1. Corporations–Finance.   2. Risk management.   3. Risk assessment.   4. Leadership.
I. Title.
  HG4026.C66 2010
  332.63'2042–dc22

                                                                    2009054379

A catalogue record for this book is available from the British Library.

ISBN 978–0–470–03264–0

Set in 10/12pt Times by Aptara, New Delhi, India

To my mother and father

Contents

Acknowledgements

Firstly, I would like to thank all the clients, both investors and investee teams, with whom I have had the pleasure of working over recent years. My appreciation goes to the many colleagues, past and present, whose support and advice have been invaluable in developing and delivering the ideas which form the basis of this book. In particular I would like to thank Andreas Buerge, Ben Dhaliwal, William Erb, Mike Hicks, Dave Irwin, Olivia Leydenfrost, Mike Smith and Professor Richard Taffler, all of whom have helped in different ways. Special thanks also go to Ian Angell, Mairi Eastwood, Mike Morgan, James Thorne and Barry Woledge at Praesta Partners, as well as Jackie Tookey. I also value the kind cooperation of Debbie Cook and Mike Ready at Compass 360 and Jackie Wagner and Wendy Lord at Hogrefe, who helped in the provision of some of the sample outputs included in the appendices. Thanks to Pete Baker, Aimee Dibbens and Karen Weller for making the publication process so enjoyable. Finally, I thank my family, in particular my sister, Jane Cooper, for their ongoing help and encouragement.

Introduction

The aim of this book is to provide a guide for investors into one of the most crucial yet opaque dimensions of any investment – the management team. This book is premised on the idea that investors should not merely focus on assessing *leadership* but that it is necessary to assess *leadership risk*. From this perspective, highlighting the strengths and weaknesses of the management team represents just one part of a broader and more sophisticated process of identifying and mapping the risks arising from the leadership agenda of the investee company, in order to provide the investor with a clear view of the management- and leadership-related factors which have the potential to create or destroy value. By framing their review of management in terms of risks it is intended that investors will be able to integrate this information with other data to provide a rich picture of the overall risk landscape of the investee business.

This book has been written during a period of unprecedented turbulence in the financial environment and, at the time of writing, the impact of this on the world of private equity remains unclear. Recent years have seen significant growth within the private equity industry. Amounts raised globally have reached hundreds of billions of dollars annually compared to tens of billions only a few years ago. The size of private equity-backed deals has also grown significantly. After several record-breaking years of deal activity, the dramatic aftermath of the credit crunch is still reverberating. It seems likely that many private equity investors will now place even greater attention on generating value from their existing portfolio of investments than seeking new deals. In any event this book will be of use.

One aspect which has not changed is the extent to which the success or failure of private equity-backed deals hinges on the performance of senior management. It is widely accepted that management is often the major contributor to value creation and destruction in private equity-backed deals. Management ultimately deliver the business strategy and produce the financial performance which will lead to a successful exit. However, the effort and attention dedicated to assessing management before and after the deal is still often very low when compared to the significant impact it can have on results.

The ability to assess management quickly and accurately is one of the key skills of the private equity investor. Moreover, the 'gut feel' which they often rely upon as the basis for assessing management has proved in many instances to give a sound basis for the investments they make. It is not the aim of this book to judge or criticise the traditional approaches which investors use when assessing leadership in their investee businesses. The intention is rather to recognise that, whilst many investors have an instinctive flair for evaluating people, they have fewer tools and frameworks at their disposal in this area than are available when they come to analyse other dimensions of a business. We address this by exploring the issues and risks associated with leadership assessment and presenting tools and approaches which can be applied in practice. Drawing on insights from this book, investors will be able to gain a clearer picture of the people dimension of their investments as a means to maximising the value which they are able to create.

THE PROBLEMS OF LEADERSHIP RISK

One central problem facing investors is that, whilst management play a crucial role in the ultimate performance of investee companies, the process through which this is achieved is complex and hard to predict. The high level of complexity surrounding management and leadership brings with it a high level of uncertainty and where there is uncertainty there is risk.

In this book, we define 'leadership risk' as:

> The risk that senior management, either individually or collectively, do not have, or fail to apply the necessary capability or motivation to deliver the expected performance and/or that their leadership of the enterprise limits or destroys value.

As leadership risk is at the heart of this book it is worthwhile to consider the key elements of this definition.

- *'Senior management'* – The contribution of the most senior team in the business (possibly the board) is seen as being central.
- *'Individually or collectively'* – Members of the senior management team have an impact as individuals and in terms of how they work with each other.
- *'Capability or motivation'* – The assessment of senior management is seen as hinging on two central questions: 'Can they do it?' and 'Will they do it?'
- *'Expected performance'* – The investor will usually have a clear sense of how they expect the business to perform on its journey to exit and this is predicated on an assumption that the management team will perform effectively.
- *'Leadership'* – Even if management do have the requisite capability and motivation, their stewardship of the enterprise – the decisions they make and where they place their energy and attention – may still have a negative impact on performance.

THE PROBLEMS OF LEADERSHIP ASSESSMENT

Having introduced the elements of leadership risk we can now look at some of the problems which make it so complex and uncertain. We will then show how these problems form the basis for the principles upon which the approach set out in this book is based.

Quantification and Measurement

Investors conduct thorough analysis when evaluating investments but leadership cannot be quantified in the same way as other dimensions of the business, such as the financial or the strategic. Leadership strengths and weakness cannot be 'measured' as such. Moreover, it is difficult, if not impossible, to identify clear causal relationships through which the strengths and weaknesses of the management team and the ultimate performance of the business are linked. This not only makes prediction difficult, it means that, even after the event, it is often difficult to 'prove' which management behaviours or characteristics led to which results.

Getting Below the Surface

Another factor which contributes to the complexity of leadership from an investor's perspective is that the key drivers of leadership effectiveness or weakness are often rooted deep below the surface. Some of the most significant issues influencing commercial success or failure will not be obvious at the time of the transaction and can remain hidden as the business is incorporated into the investment portfolio. As well as being hard for the investor to identify, these may also be difficult for the management team themselves to understand. Investors are obliged to impute the suitability and capability of leaders on the basis of interviews, discussions and track record. However, future performance will be equally, if not more, influenced by inner hopes, fears, beliefs and motivations, of which even the individual concerned may not be aware.

The Effect of Being Assessed

A further layer of complexity stems from the likelihood that, in contrast to other, more impersonal, areas assessed by investors, the very act of assessing the leadership team can influence the results of that assessment. When leaders know they are being assessed, they will have a strong incentive to 'be on their best behaviour'. The very fact that a leadership team is being assessed, particularly in such a high-stakes scenario, will influence the way they perform. As a result, it is not possible for the investor, in their capacity as assessor of the leadership team, to be entirely independent of the assessment process.

Deal Jeopardy

Further problems can also arise because, if leadership assessment forms part of the pre-deal due diligence, it is often conducted at a point in the investment process when pressure is at a peak and the stakes are at their highest. There may be constraints such as lack of time and lack of access to the senior team. Investors are keenly aware of the risk that leadership assessment may be unduly intrusive and may sour the relationship between the investor and the leadership team and even jeopardise the deal itself. These and other concerns mean that, while not disputing the central role which management can play in creating and destroying value, investors approach management due diligence with considerable caution.

THE PRINCIPLES UNDERPINNING THIS BOOK

The problems described above provide the basis for the principles upon which this book has been written. The framework which is summarised below and explained in detail in the following chapters is intended to address the complexities of leadership assessment by providing a process which has depth and rigour and will enhance rather than tarnish the relationship with the leadership team under assessment.

Process and Structure

The first principle is that leadership assessment should be conducted in a thorough and systematic manner. The framework set out in the following chapters is based around a four-stage process.

> **Prepare** – To ensure adequate preparation it is important to:
> - Establish in advance what information is required from the assessment and how this information will be used.
> - Have a clear plan setting out the timetable for the assessment and specifying who will be assessing whom and in what timeframe.
> - Identify and remain vigilant to factors which could influence the objectivity and accuracy of the assessment.
>
> **Assess** – Conduct the assessment with rigour and ensure it is as objective as possible. It is important to make a distinction between data gathering and data evaluation. Assessors should not attempt to conduct these steps simultaneously.
>
> **Review** – Consider the data gathered in a systematic and impartial manner and evaluate it in the light of the wider business agenda, other dimensions of the business and the potential impact on business performance.
>
> **Address** – Translate the findings of the review into plans and actions. Have clear criteria for deciding which are high- and low-priority issues and set out a clear plan of how these will be dealt with.

Assess at Multiple Levels

The definition of leadership risk refers to the impact of leadership behaviour, both individually and collectively. We suggest that leadership assessment should embrace three levels:

- The individual level;
- The team level; and
- The business or organisational level.

Multiple Perspectives

Given the complexities associated with leadership, no single data source can be expected to suffice in its assessment. We therefore suggest that data relating to different dimensions of leadership be collected from a number of different sources and then compared and triangulated in order to build a rich picture. Specifically, we suggest that data is gathered from the perspective of 'self', 'others' and 'context'.

Depth of Awareness

The four-step process described above ensures that the assessment process is conducted in a systematic and thorough manner. In order to ensure that the assessment is as effective as possible, the investor has to look beyond the plan and take account of what is happening below the surface. In most areas of business analysis and due diligence, the focus is on the outer world (the observable, reportable dimension) of the investee business. Whilst this level of analysis is important, when it comes to assessing leadership this is not sufficient. As we will set out in later chapters, it is also important to remain aware of the influence of what is going on below the surface (which we will refer to as the 'inner world') of both the investee AND the investor.

Figure I.1 indicates just some of the factors which can play a role in effectiveness on these dimensions.

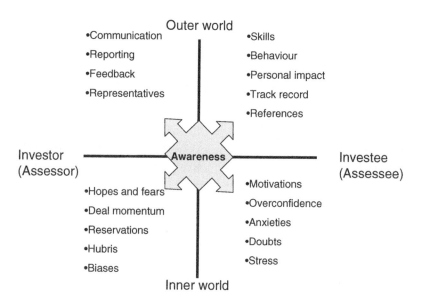

Figure I.1   Factors influencing effectiveness

Remember the Relationship

We referred above to the concern that leadership assessment may damage the relationship between investor and investee. It is therefore essential that the assessment is conducted in a manner which, as far as possible, will strengthen this relationship. Here, clear communication about purpose and process is essential. If conducted properly, leadership assessment can be a means by which an investor can differentiate themselves positively from their competition and maximise the chances of the success of the transaction.

It is critical that the investor remains vigilant and self-aware and appreciates the impact they are having.

Assessment is the Beginning of a Process

A further important consideration is that leadership assessment should focus more on the future than on the past. Achieving the growth which private equity and strategic investors are looking for is predicated on significant challenge and change for the investee management team. It is possible, and even likely, that the skills and abilities which enabled the management team to grow their business to its current state will be different from the skills required to take it to the next level and achieve the satisfactory exit. Rather than a single 'snapshot', which forms the basis for a one-off decision (as can be the case with financial or strategic due diligence), leadership assessment should form the first step in an ongoing process of understanding and addressing the leadership agenda upon which business success is based. The aim is that the issues identified are monitored on an ongoing basis and plans put in place to address them are fine-tuned in the light of experience.

THE AUDIENCE FOR THIS BOOK

This book is intended to be a practical guide for private equity and other strategic investors. Leadership risk is a serious issue for all businesses and, indeed, all organisations. However, in the case of private equity investors or other investors making a substantial strategic investment in another business, certain factors raise the significance of leadership risk even further:

- Given the challenging growth targets often associated with such investments, significant change is implied for the investee business, which also implies significant change and challenge for the leadership team.

- Once the investor has made the investment, it is a material event for both parties and changes the world or both the investor and investee.
- The investor will have the necessary access and control to conduct an in-depth leadership risk assessment.
- The investor will have sufficient influence to be able to drive, or at least influence changes and decisions based on the result of the risk assessment.

The tone and language used assume that the reader is already familiar with the world of corporate finance. In contrast to this, the principles and frameworks relating to the assessment of leadership risk are presented in a way which does not presuppose significant prior knowledge. The terms 'investor' and 'private equity investor' are used to refer to representatives of the business making the investment who negotiate and execute deals. 'Investee' relates to the leadership team of the business which is being invested in.

The book will also be of interest and value to a much wider range of businesses which are not engaging in, or subject to, investment. At the start of the book, we point out that understanding leadership-related risk takes on a special significance in environments where there is growing complexity and/or rapid change. The ideas presented here will therefore be helpful to any business experiencing rapid growth and striving for ambitious targets, in which success or failure hinges on effective leadership and any assessment or leadership development activities must be very focused and closely related to business success.

The following chapters draw on insights drawn from a range of theoretical sources, including leadership research, organisational and individual psychology, and also reflect the author's own experience of applying these in practice. Approaches are presented in practical rather than theoretical terms so that they may be readily applied in real-life situations.

It is intended that readers of this book may draw on it as a resource to support them in addressing a number of issues relating to leadership assessment within the context of reviewing businesses in their existing portfolio or conducting pre-deal leadership due diligence. Issues covered include:

- Identifying what needs to be done at each stage.
- Planning and managing the process.

- Enabling the investor to make the best possible use of whatever time and access to the leadership team is available.
- Highlighting and addressing issues relating to planning and managing leadership due diligence.
- Communicating the process to existing and prospective leadership teams undergoing assessment.
- Evaluating and selecting third-party providers who may support the leadership assessment process.
- Using and integrating the findings of the leadership risk assessment to maximise success on the route to exit.

Where appropriate lists of representative skills, characteristics and issues are presented, this is done for illustrative purposes. None of the lists presented should be interpreted as representing a 'universal' or exclusive checklist. Throughout the book we emphasise the importance of context and assessing specific leaders in their own terms within the specific context of the business they are leading, so there can be no universal checklists.

THE STRUCTURE OF THIS BOOK

In Chapter 1 we consider the risk landscape in which leadership risk assessment takes place and develop the themes and principles summarised above in greater depth. In Chapter 2 we introduce the elements of the four-stage leadership risk mapping model and begin to build a high-level map of the assessment process. Chapter 3 is concerned with the first stage of the model – planning and preparation – and we set out techniques which can be used to plot the critical leadership path to exit and show how this can be used to specify what needs to be assessed. The following chapters cover the assessment process itself. Chapter 4 looks at how to decide what should be assessed at an individual level and Chapter 5 looks at how to actually approach individual-level assessment. Chapter 6 explores how to decide what to assess at a team level and Chapter 7 looks at how to conduct team-level assessment. Chapters 8 and 9 deal with assessment at an organisational or business level. Chapter 10 deals with the process of analysing and interpreting the results of the assessment and producing a high-level map which charts key elements of leadership risk. Chapter 11 describes how to address the results of the review and sets out the principles of translating these into development plans so as to ensure that the insights generated

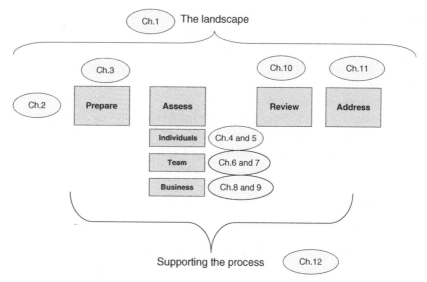

Figure I.2 Chapter overview

by the process inform the ongoing leadership and success of the business. Finally, Chapter 12 covers the potential use of third-party consultants and provides a snapshot of the market place for relevant services. See Figure I.2 for a graphical representation of the book's structure.

1
The Landscape of Leadership Risk

1.1 INTRODUCTION

One of the central ideas upon which this book is based is that, in order for private equity investors to maximise the chances of creating value in their investee companies, it is better to focus on assessing 'leadership risk' rather than simply assess 'leadership'. Although the distinction between leadership and leadership risk may seem a minor one, it is in fact highly significant. The assessment of leadership is a fairly narrow activity focused on certain key individuals whereas leadership risk is much broader and takes as its starting point the chain of value creation and destruction. Whilst the primary emphasis of this book is related to *how* leadership risk can be assessed and managed, the current chapter sets the scene by considering the question of *why* leadership risk represents the problem it does. Before introducing the leadership risk mapping framework, which is described in detail in the following chapters, the current chapter is therefore dedicated to a consideration of the landscape of leadership risk which confronts private equity investors and the problem of how best to make sense of that landscape.

We will argue that, to manage risk of any kind it is important to minimise uncertainty and raise awareness of the variables which may enhance or inhibit success. To make effective decisions it is essential to have a broad and deep understanding of the territory in which one is operating. This is critical in providing the insight required to ask the right questions and identify which areas require attention. It can be argued that the most serious risks facing any business are those which are not already in the awareness of the management team or stakeholders. In such situations, where the boundaries of the risk map are too narrowly drawn, there is a false sense of certainty and security. Several of the dimensions of leadership risk which will be explored in subsequent chapters fall into this category.

Irrespective of the particulars of a specific investment, there are two general problems associated with leadership and leadership risk which often arise in the context of private equity-backed businesses. Firstly, in rapidly growing businesses, the future is always different from the past and, ultimately, the extent to which the business is able to anticipate and adapt comes down to leadership. When unexpected leadership issues manifest without prior awareness or preparation and there is insufficient time to explore these in sufficient depth, decisions may be taken which lead to extreme or inappropriate measures. Secondly, in fast growing businesses, leadership assessment and development is often seen as a low priority and does not appear on the investor's 'dashboard' as being a significant dimension through which the business is driven. As a result, the topic of leadership often begins to attract attention only when it becomes a problem. Significant leadership-related decisions may therefore be rushed and made on the basis of an inadequate understanding of the links between business performance and leadership. When such decisions are rushed in this way it becomes difficult to evaluate the possible consequences, or other possible options in any depth. We will explore the problems related to rushed leadership-related decisions further in Chapter 2.

We begin this chapter with a critical examination of the 'dominant lens' which is used to understand business – that of accounting language. We will highlight some of the many advantages which accounting representations offer whilst also indicating some of the limitations of this perspective. In particular, we will suggest that the apparent rationality of accounting is much less robust under conditions of rapid change, complexity and uncertainty – which are the conditions surrounding many private equity investments. We will also explore the issue of uncertainty further and its links with the history of the development of the idea of risk. Having identified some of the problems arising from the use of accounting under conditions of risk and uncertainty, we will also consider why the leadership agenda associated with private equity-backed businesses often poses a particular problem. Having set out the limitations of both an accounting perspective and a leadership perspective we will then make the case for using the leadership risk framework, not as a means of managing risk in a formal sense but as a useful metaphor for identifying and addressing some of the critical issues which can create or destroy value in private equity-backed businesses.

1.2   THE FINANCIAL PERSPECTIVE

Accounting is widely recognised as being the 'language of business' and financial data will always be the central reference point on a private equity investor's 'dashboard'. Financial analysis supports decisions about which opportunities to explore, which investments to make and how much to pay. An understanding of the numbers guides the many decisions made both by the investor and the investee management team on the journey through to exit. The accounting view is so dominant that it is taken for granted. However, but for the purpose of the current discussion it is useful to examine the characteristics of accounting which make it so appealing, and highlighting some of the critical functions which accounting language performs:

- Enabling communication – accounting represents a highly convenient 'universal shorthand' which enables the quick and straightforward description and communication of widely differing scenarios in equivalent terms.
- Establishing a sense of order – accounting creates a clear sense of balance, order and structure and so forms the basis for 'rational' management and control.
- Reducing complexity – the way in which accounting achieves the above functions is by reducing complexity and, in reducing complexity, creating a greater sense of certainty.
- Managing the 'problem' of time – underpinning the above functions of accounting, the way it solves the problem of time which is described below.

One of the central themes of the current chapter is the link between complexity, uncertainty and risk. A central challenge facing a private equity investor is how to make decisions about a business as it moves from a 'known' past into an 'unknown' future. To understand and manage risk it is necessary to view what is known in the present in terms of its future implications. Indeed, it could be argued that the basis for successful business planning and management is rooted in a view of the business which unites past, present and future. Businesses are able to achieve precisely such a view through the use of accounting systems.

The language of accounting reduces past and future business events to equivalent terms, linking them seamlessly and giving a sense of continuity. Beyond that, it offers the enticing possibility of playing with time. Alternative accounting treatments can provide alternative accounts of the past. They can also be used to generate an infinite range of future scenarios. Accounting systems present the past, present and future in a consistent way with financial statements and management accounts showing what has gone before and business plans and budgets indicating what is to come; both time periods are expressed in equivalent terms. Any given moment – past, present or future – can be frozen and expressed in terms of assets and liabilities in a balance sheet. The objective and impartial flavour of accounting language makes it an ideal framework upon which to build a 'rational' view of the world.

Accounting therefore provides a guideline for rational management, reduces complexity and provides a sense of order. However, this sense of certainty comes at a price and so brings with it a number of problems, not the least of which is the simplification entailed in translating the complexities and uncertainties of business reality into the neat order of numbers. For over half a century, researchers have suggested that, in practice, accounting frameworks are used in different ways depending on the level of uncertainty which prevails. In situations where the business being accounted for is relatively stable and there is a high degree of clarity about the cause and effect relationships which create value, accounting lends itself well to the function of building understanding and making decisions. However, the more rapid the rate of change in a business, the greater the difference between its past and future and the more complexity there is, the less useful accounting language is as a basis for making decisions and making sense of the business. Here, although accounting provides the same sense of order, what is actually happening is a process of post hoc rationalisation. Major decisions have to be made on the basis of incomplete or ambiguous information and only afterwards can any degree of certainty be achieved. The scenario confronting private equity-backed investment teams and the general partners who invest in them almost always involves significant change and uncertainty. The closer one gets to this scenario, the more decisions are based on 'leadership inspiration'. As a result, a proper understanding of 'leadership' becomes more important as the basis for understanding and managing the business.

From this perspective, it can be argued that when it comes to understanding and managing risk, the value of an accounting frame of reference decreases as the rate of change and the degree of complexity increase (see Figure 1.1)

1.3   A BRIEF HISTORY OF RISK AND UNCERTAINTY

The issue of risk and uncertainty and the distinction between the two extends well beyond the world of accounting and it is useful here to consider briefly how these themes have developed over time. Over the

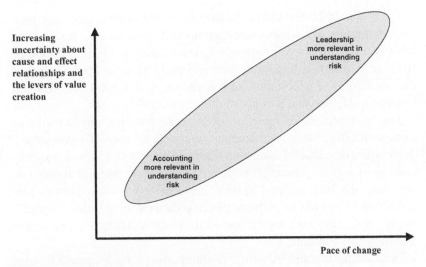

Figure 1.1   Accounting, risk and uncertainty

centuries, human beings have responded in differing ways when confronted with the inevitable uncertainty of events and the consequences
of decisions. There has been a general tendency to assume that things
which are more readily quantifiable are more important than things
which are more nebulous and subjective; and more time is devoted to
analysing those aspects which are quantifiable than those which are not.
By their nature, investment decisions revolve around uncertainty and
risk and it is important for investors to recognise the boundary between
the quantifiable and the unknown. In his book *Against the Gods*, Peter
Bernstein notes: 'Today, we rely less on superstition and tradition than
people did in the past, not because we are more rational, but because
our understanding of risk enables us to make decisions in a rational
mode.'

A key distinction, highlighted by the economist Frank Knight early
in the 20th century, is that between risk and uncertainty. The statistical
frameworks which had been developed in the preceding centuries were
often too firmly rooted in the analysis of probability applied to games
of chance, such as roulette or dice. In this context, probabilities can
be established with some precision, and risk assessments can be made.
However, in business and the wider economy, there will always be
factors that are unknown, unquantifiable and unexpected. For all the
apparent rigour and scientific method in applying probability theories

to the real world, they are essentially irrational to the extent that they exclude factors which cannot be quantified. Knight wrote: 'Uncertainty must be taken in a sense radically distinct from the familiar notion of risk, from which it has never been properly separate. It will appear that a measurable uncertainty, or risk proper, is so far different from an immeasurable one that it is not in effect uncertainty at all.'

The ever-present element of surprise means that any attempt to extrapolate from the past frequency of events is inherently dangerous. Techniques developed from areas where probabilities can be accurately calculated may be pleasingly neat, but that does not mean that they can automatically be translated to other areas merely because data can be generated to be able to perform the calculations. In the real economic world, even if certain patterns appear to be stable, there is no guarantee that they will continue.

In a similar manner, Knight's contemporary John Maynard Keynes argued that the probabilities of events in the real world are not subject to tools of measurement. In 1937, in *The General Theory*, Keynes wrote: 'The game of roulette is not subject to uncertainty. The sense that I use the term is that in which the prospect of a European war is uncertain, or the price of copper and the rate of interest 20 years' hence, or the obsolescence of a new invention. About these matters, there is no scientific basis on which to form any calculable probability whatever. We simply do not know.'

Keynes was scathing about the reliance of classical economics on past events, arguing that the unstable and dynamic nature of an economy means that the mathematical patterns established in the recent past may have little or no relevance today, as the underlying context has changed, and the players never have perfect information.

The implication of this dimension of risk – or more accurately defined, uncertainty – is that a different kind of assessment is needed. In business contexts there has traditionally been a bias towards managing and analysing aspects of the company that are measured, over those that are harder to quantify but may be equally influential. However, the true measure of a robust risk management framework is not the depth and complexity of analysis it generates but the extent to which it can embrace and facilitate understanding of those factors which ultimately influence performance and can create or destroy value.

The distinction between risk and uncertainty is perhaps at its most stark in the area of leadership risk Leadership risk is uncertain and complex because it relates people and their capacity to lead businesses, and this is a complex and uncertain process. Although leadership can have a significant impact on business performance, the mechanism by which this occurs is opaque so that precise causal relationships cannot be discerned. As a result, predictions cannot be made and probabilities cannot be calculated. Moreover, the drivers of human behaviour, actions and reactions lie below the surface and may not even be within the awareness of those concerned. As we will set out in the final section of this chapter, such problems are not insurmountable and the leadership risk mapping framework described in the rest of this book can provide a way forward.

The above discussion suggests that the value of accounting, as a means of truly managing and understanding business and risk, diminishes as uncertainty and complexity increase and, indeed, the whole issue of the distinction between risk and uncertainty is problematic. It can be argued that, the more uncertainty there is surrounding a business, the more the success or failure of that business hinges on the leadership capability of the senior team but, as we will explore below, the whole concept of 'leadership' also represents something of a problem.

1.4   LEADERSHIP THEORY

The previous section suggested that the conditions of change and complexity associated with private equity investments are such that an understanding of leadership is of key importance and that the language of accounting, the predominant 'lens' used to understand business, is ill-equipped to provide useful insights in this area. A further problem is that there is no equivalent universal 'language' for tracking and managing issues relating to leadership risk. The literature on leadership is diverse and, arguably, inconclusive. Just as accounting language can be seen to be problematic, so can the language of leadership, and some of the associated problems are set out below.

Firstly, leadership assessment and development is often seen as peripheral to the main business agenda. It is seen as a worthy activity to engage in when sufficient time and resources are available but it is really something which larger, more stable organisations can address and not a central topic within the context of private equity investments. One reason for this is that the leadership behaviour agenda is not sufficiently rooted in the business context – it is seen as being too general and too abstract. Many leadership development courses are only intermittently relevant and contain components which will not be used. This perception will be reinforced by the personal experience of many private equity investors who have completed an MBA. For many, the value of an MBA lies in its demonstration that the individual has gained entry and survived in the highly competitive environment of a high-prestige business school rather than the actual knowledge acquired. As a result the actual content of the programme, particularly in the area of leadership theory, is often forgotten.

The framework described in subsequent chapters of this book is not about presenting an ideal type of leadership or adopting a new persona, but about raising awareness in those areas where increased attention will take leadership to the next level and so boost business performance.

1.5   LEADERSHIP RISK AND UNCERTAINTY

In the Introduction we defined leadership risk as follows:

> The risk that senior management, either individually or collectively, do not have, or fail to apply the necessary capability or motivation to deliver the expected performance and/or that their leadership of the enterprise limits or destroys value.

In light of the previous section it is clear that leadership risk does not represent 'risk' in any formal sense as it is not possible to calculate probabilities in the areas of leadership behaviours. However, it can be argued that the use of the term 'leadership risk' and the use of a 'leadership risk mapping framework' are useful if 'risk' is understood in a metaphorical rather than a formal sense. The advantages of a risk mapping metaphor are described below.

1.5.1   Emphasis on the 'Asset'

Thinking in terms of 'risk' brings attention to the fact that there is an 'asset' which holds the potential to generate value in the future. This encourages the investor to constantly look and think ahead and reflect on issues such as how the potential of that asset will be realised. This helps to sharpen focus and helps to ensure that attention is given to the question of what will create and destroy value in the business.

1.5.2 Systematic

Using a risk metaphor helps to ensure that the business is explored in a systematic and disciplined manner. This kind of systematic perspective is useful because it brings attention to the way in which threats, opportunities and other invariables are interconnected. A risk management framework therefore enhances awareness of how these factors are connected rather than looking at them in isolation.

1.5.3 Structured

Exploring issues from a risk management perspective helps to ensure an approach which is structured and disciplined. As we will see further in the next chapter, it helps to achieve balance and rigorous understanding and ensures that issues are worked through in a methodical manner.

1.5.4 Prioritisation

Use of a risk management metaphor helps to provide a basis for considering issues in equivalent terms, which helps to ensure that priorities are clearly set.

1.5.5 Decision Making

The structure provided by the risk management framework also provides a sound basis for making important decisions. It helps to ensure that the decision maker is well prepared to make important decisions and is able to act quickly and confidently when the need arises. It thereby reduces the likelihood of unexpected threats manifesting.

1.6 LEADERSHIP RISK IN BUSINESS PERFORMANCE

To manage leadership risk successfully it is important to identify as clearly and systematically as possible the links between leadership performance and business performance. A useful starting point in understanding leadership performance is the work of Timothy Gallwey, who initially looked at how to improve performance in sport and then went on to show how similar principles could be applied to the world of work. Gallwey's work centres on what he refers to as the 'inner game', at the heart of which is a simple formula relating to human performance:

$$Performance = Potential - Interference$$

We will show that this formula has significant implications for leadership risk. Working though the framework which is set out in subsequent chapters makes it possible to unpack the two variables of potential and interference in order to ensure that the performance of the leadership team is as effective as possible, which in turn will maximise the chances of achieving business success. In introducing the formula it is useful to consider the significance of each term in the inner game equation from a leadership risk perspective.

1.6.1   'Performance'

Performance relates to what the members of the management team, both individually and collectively, actually do. In essence, this relates to the way they lead the business. It relates to the decisions they make, the extent to which they motivate and inspire their people, the way they manage one another and their relationships with key stakeholders and the way they interact with the investor. Their 'performance' in the management team as leaders will be directly linked to the 'performance' of the business. However, whereas business performance is ultimately an outcome expressed in accounting terms – '*what* results has the business produced?', leadership performance relates to the more complex question of *how* those results are achieved. Performance, then, relates to whatever it is the leadership team actually does, and the essence of leadership risk is to understand the factors which drive the performance.

1.6.2   'Potential'

The potential of the leadership team relates to how far they actually possess the requisite knowledge, skill and experience to lead the business to a successful exit. From a leadership risk perspective this factor in the equation centres on the question 'Can they do it?' The assessment techniques described in subsequent chapters attempt to gauge the depth of potential on which the management team can draw. Where gaps exist between the potential of the management team and the requirements of the business, this can form the basis of the leadership development plan. However, to fully maximise business performance such a development plan also needs to take full account of the final element of the equation – interference.

1.6.3 'Interference'

The third element of Gallwey's equation, interference, is arguably the most opaque and most often overlooked, and the leadership mapping framework attempts to address this. Interference relates to any factors which could get in the way of the leadership team realising their full potential and which could therefore impede business performance. Although some sources of interference may be obvious, many are not and can only be identified through a process of careful exploration. Sources of interference may exist within the minds of the management team and could include factors such as their level of motivation and clarity of understanding. Other sources of interference may stem from the limit of human capabilities (for example, from exhaustion). However, interference is not solely located within the leadership team. Problems may arise in the relationship between the investor and the investee teams which may impede performance. As we will see in Chapter 8, interference may also arise on a wider organisational or cultural level, for example where there is resistance to change.

One reason that the 'inner game' model is particularly relevant for private equity-backed businesses is that it deals with learning and how best to facilitate learning. Given the complexity and rapid change associated with private equity-backed businesses, the challenge of managing and leading these will almost inevitably require the senior leadership team to learn and develop in some way. As we will explore further in the next chapter, problems can arise when either the members of the management team themselves, or the investor, attempt to bypass this learning process and either 'teach' or impose solutions. As we shall see, rather than 'solving' leadership weaknesses, this approach may compound the problems which it attempts to address. The alternative put forward in the leadership risk mapping framework is to follow three key principles which Timothy Gallwey found to be highly significant in learning and development. The first, and possibly the most significant, of these is the importance of raising *awareness* and doing this in a nonjudgemental way. As described further in the following sections, the framework is built upon techniques which raise awareness on a number of levels. The second of Gallwey's key principles is to *trust* in the inner potential of the leaders in the business. Gallwey found that learning takes place quite naturally merely through the process of raising awareness. For the purpose of the current discussion, the important thing to bear in mind is that both the investor and the investee management team need to maintain faith in the ability of the management team to learn appropriately in light of the insights which come from raising awareness. The final one of Gallwey's principles is to keep the *choice* with the choice maker. In the case of private equity-backed businesses, this means that the investor should resist the temptation to dictate approaches and solutions and allow the leaders of the business to decide for themselves what to do. As long as both parties have a clear shared understanding of the ultimate outcomes which are sought, and awareness is raised appropriately, this should maximise the chances of success.

Of the three principles set out above, awareness is probably the most significant within the context of management risk mapping. Throughout the following chapters we will emphasise the importance of maintaining awareness on a number of dimensions using the model described below.

1.7   THE FOUR QUADRANTS OF AWARENESS

At the beginning of this chapter we suggested that the essence of effective risk management was the reduction of uncertainty. Effective risk management therefore begins with the raising of awareness of whichever factors may ultimately influence success or failure. In the previous section we began to set out the high-level elements of leadership risk and we will now develop this idea further by introducing a model of awareness which underpins the framework set out in subsequent chapters. Given the complexity and subtlety of leadership risk it is important not to oversimplify and to be aware that factors influencing value creation and destruction may or may not be obvious on the surface. For this reason, the first dimension of this model relates to the inner and outer world. The outer world relates elements which are observable and, to a certain extent, measurable. This includes factors such as behaviour, systems, processes and policies. The inner world relates to what is going on below the surface on an emotional and psychological level in the minds of those involved. This includes factors such as knowledge, emotions, hopes and fears. The other dimension of the model relates to the two stakeholder groups most directly affected by leadership risk, the investor and the investee. It is important to maintain awareness of this dimension as, if it is the investor who is conducting the assessment of leadership risk in the investee management team, then they need to

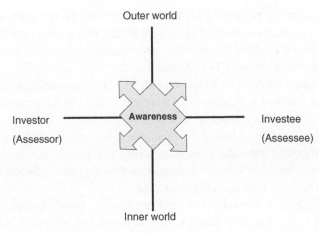

Figure 1.2   The four quadrants of awareness

remain aware that they are not independent of the process. As mentioned earlier, the mere fact that one is being assessed in itself influences the result of that assessment. Given the tensions and pressures surrounding private equity-backed businesses it is vital that the assessment of leadership risk is done in a way which enhances rather than impairs the relationship between investor and investee, so maintaining an awareness of the relationship between the two and the impact of one party's actions of the other is critical. In a wider context this dimension can also be equated to whoever is conducting the assessment (the 'assessor') and whoever is being assessed ('the assessee'). Taking these two dimensions, it is possible to identify the four quadrants and these are shown in Figure 1.2.

Throughout the remaining chapters we will return to the relevant factors arising in each of these quadrants and look at how a fair consideration of the interplay between them can greatly enhance one's insight into leadership risk and ensure that the process of assessing it is as painless and effective as possible.

1.8 SUMMARY

- To be truly effective, it is important that a company's risk map embraces all the factors which can influence success or failure. The biggest risks of all are the ones that do not appear on the risk map.

- Leadership risk presents a particular problem in private equity-backed businesses because the rate of change means that a great deal depends on effective leadership, yet leadership assessment and development are not seen as being a high priority.
- Accounting works well as the language of business, acting as a guideline for rational management. However, it does this by presenting a highly simplified version of reality.
- As uncertainty increases in the business, it becomes harder and harder to extrapolate from the past, accounting is less and less useful as a true guideline for 'rational management' and tends to be used more as a vehicle of post hoc rationalisation.
- The distinction between risk and uncertainty is often blurred. In a formal sense it is only possible to talk about risk when all outcomes can be defined and probabilities calculated.
- Leadership risk is associated with significant uncertainty because it depends on human behaviour, which cannot be predicted.
- Leadership theory does not provide an alternative to accounting. It is often difficult to reconcile the leadership agenda with the business agenda.
- One way to approach this is to think in terms of leadership risk and use risk as a metaphor to frame the various issues and factors which can impact business performance from a leadership perspective.
- In exploring the link between leadership risk and business performance, the formula: 'Performance = Potential − Interference' is helpful.
- It is also useful to cultivate awareness in four dimensions: the outer world of the investee, the outer world of the investor, the inner world of the investee and the inner world of the investor.
- This 'four quadrants of awareness' framework underpins much of the leadership risk framework. The aim is not just to raise awareness in the four quadrants, but also to consider how they relate to each other.

REFERENCES

Bernstein, P. 1996. *Against the Gods: the Remarkable Story of Risk*, John Wiley & Sons, Ltd.

Gallwey, T. 2000. *The Inner Game of Work, Overcoming mental obstacles for maximum performance*, Orien Business.

Keynes, J.M. 1937. *The General Theory of Employment, Interest and Money*, Palgrave Macmillan.

2

Overview of the Leadership Risk
Mapping Framework

2.1 INTRODUCTION

In the previous chapter we looked at the way in which leadership risk can be of critical importance in determining the success or failure of private equity investments and began to introduce some of the concepts and principles which can be used to make sense of leadership risk. The purpose of this chapter is to introduce an integrated framework for mapping and managing leadership risk, and the various elements of the framework which form the basis of subsequent chapters. The framework described below is intended to enhance rather than replace the techniques traditionally used by private equity investors, many of whom have an instinctive sense of how to anticipate, identify and address issues with the leadership of their investee businesses. The framework aims to strike a balance between two principal considerations. Firstly, it seeks to be practical, useful and pragmatic so as to ensure that relevant issues can be identified and addressed as quickly and efficiently as possible. Secondly, it aims to achieve this whilst still going into sufficient depth to recognise adequately the complexities of leadership risk. It represents a systematic approach which can be followed by investors and/or investee management teams to arrive at the most accurate and useful answers to the following questions:

- What leadership performance is required to arrive at the business outcomes which we are seeking?
- Do the leadership team, individually and collectively, have the potential to deliver that performance? If not, what can be done to address any gaps?
- Are there any factors which may inhibit their ability to perform to their potential?

We have discussed the complex and unquantifiable nature of leadership risk and this complexity represents a considerable challenge for anyone attempting to understand or manage it. When looking at how best to negotiate the complexity of leadership risk it is useful to consider the law of requisite variety which comes from General Systems Theory and was proposed by William Ashby. This law states that for one system to be capable of controlling or managing another it must be of the same or greater level of complexity. For the purposes of the current discussion, this would imply that for an investor to have a leadership risk mapping system capable of dealing with the leadership team of a business, that system would need to be as complex and have as many options and variables as the leadership team itself. In practice, trying to create a framework with such a high level of sophistication would be completely unrealistic and it would also be risky for an investor to even imagine that their approach to assessing leadership risk could even come close to dealing with the underlying level of complexity. The proposal made in this book is that, rather than aim for a single, overly complex system to facilitate leadership risk assessment, the investor should use a range of systems and approaches and gather data from a range of sources.

The framework addresses this problem in three ways. Firstly, it assesses leadership on different levels: the level of the individual leaders, the level of the leadership team and finally by looking at leadership issues which exist throughout the business on a cultural level. Secondly, it draws on several sources of data so, for each of these levels, the framework gathers data and raises awareness through reference to multiple perspectives, which means that data can be triangulated and the existence of emerging themes can be validated. Thirdly, it follows a disciplined, systematic process to ensure that rash interventions are avoided.

These aspects of the framework are described in greater detail below.

2.1.1   Multiple Levels

As mentioned above, one way to address the complexity surrounding leadership risk is to break 'leadership' into different component parts.

The first point of reference, and arguably the most significant, is that of the individual members of the leadership team. Approaches to assessment traditionally used by private equity investors are focused on individuals, and individual skills and behaviours are perhaps the easiest to describe and assess. The 'leadership' of the business is effectively embodied in the individual members of the management team and investors are naturally inclined to relate to leaders on an individual level. The second level of analysis used in the framework is that of the senior leadership team, seen as a collective entity. From a leadership risk point of view, this level of analysis is extremely important. Ideally, operating as a team enables the individual leaders to leverage one another's strengths and compensate for one another's weaknesses so that the management team becomes greater than the sum of its parts. However, a weak team may be so dysfunctional as to inhibit and impair performance, producing worse results than if the individual members were to operate in isolation. The team level is also important because it is often in this forum that many key business decisions are made and challenges addressed. The final, and perhaps the most opaque, level of analysis used in the framework is that of the organisation as a whole. Whilst many would acknowledge that organisational culture can play a critical role in influencing business performance, the mechanisms through which it can be led or influenced are often hard to discern. By encouraging an exploration of the organisational and cultural factors which may enhance or inhibit business performance, the framework aims to ensure that relevant issues on this level are at least identified and so find a way onto the wider risk map.

2.1.2 Multiple Perspectives

As discussed in the previous chapter, leadership risk does not lend itself easily to measurement and quantification. The mapping of leadership risk is, by its nature, more descriptive than evaluative. Because 'objective' measures are not feasible, it can be difficult to form a clear view and establish a solid basis for conclusions and decisions. For this reason, the framework takes data from a number of sources which can then be compared and triangulated in order to test understanding. The principal perspectives used in the framework are as follows:

- *The 'self', or inner perspective* – This perspective is used for individuals and teams where the subject of the assessment is interrogated to give their own evaluation of themself. For example, individuals may be required to complete questionnaires or psychometric tools, or team maps can be compiled by aggregating the perspectives of individual team members.
- *The 'others', or outer perspective* – This perspective comes from other parties and stakeholders who have direct experience of the subject of the assessment and are therefore able to make an evaluation of it and reflect upon the impact it has upon them. In the case of

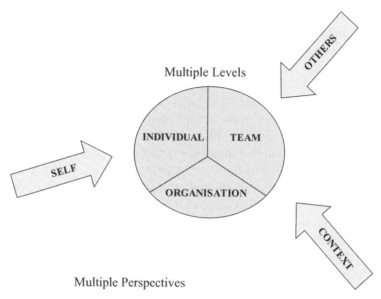

Figure 2.1   Principal perspectives

individuals this may involve gathering feedback from other members of the team, and on a team level may involve team questionnaires.

- *The 'context', or surrounding perspective* – This relates to the wider environment in which the subject is operating. The notion of context can be very broad and may include the role and responsibilities of the person or people being assessed, their goals and objectives and/or the specific challenges they face.

See Figure 2.1 for a graphical overview.

2.1.3   Systematic Process

The stages of the framework are described in detail in the following section. Before exploring these, it is useful to consider the different scenarios relating to leadership issues which can play out if a systematic approach is not adopted and, instead, an ad hoc approach is adopted, driven by the presenting issues. This can be illustrated by examining some possible scenarios and their consequences.

Scenario 1 – The Business Faces a Crisis or an Unexpected Threat

In this situation, a common tendency is for the investor to impose a solution and act as a 'rescuer' or 'teacher' to the investee leadership team. Although it may provide a remedy in the short term, this approach brings with it a number of potential problems and risks. Firstly, such a reaction is often focused primarily on symptoms and outcomes rather than the underlying causes. Because this solution is also often imposed when there is considerable time pressure on all parties involved, this may limit the extent to which the presenting issue can be understood in depth and can mean that underlying risks go unaddressed. Secondly, such a dynamic can build a sense of dependency between the investee leadership team and the investor. It may also contribute to an atmosphere of distrust. Finally, such an approach often makes inefficient use of both the investor's time and the time of the investee leadership team.

Scenario 2 – Perceived Confusion Arising from Complex Problems

Where the investor perceives there to be confusion on the part of the investee leadership team or they are struggling to dissect the complex problem, a common temptation is for the investor to intercede to remedy this by providing apparent clarity and explanation. However, this may involve an oversimplification on the part of the investor and they may be tempted to make assumptions and impose meanings based on previous experience. Consequences of this approach may include the management team and the investor reaching a false sense of apparent understanding, although the specifics and complexities of the situation still go unaddressed. There is also a risk that consequences and implications are not fully considered in the rush to reach understanding and resolution. In deciding on next steps there is a greater risk that responsibilities and accountabilities are not properly thought through and allocated.

Scenario 3 – Conflict

When conflict arises in the leadership team the investor may be tempted to intercede and act as a referee. They may pathologise the conflict, seeing it as something which is wholly negative and must be removed as quickly as possible or they may choose to ignore it. One problem arising from this is that the benefits of the conflict are never realised. Moreover, the situation may become framed in terms of winners and losers, leading to lasting resentment and increasing the chance of the same conflict resurfacing in the future. Finally, there is also a risk that if conflict is seen as something bad and unhealthy it becomes suppressed in the future, with the result that issues and challenges are suppressed rather than explored openly.

Scenario 4 – Perceived Lack of Capacity in the Leadership Team

Where the leadership team is seen as being in some way deficient or not performing, the investor may frame this in terms of weaknesses and make snap decisions, possibly involving a reallocation of responsibilities and even firing key individuals in certain instances. In cases of underperformance there is a tendency to focus on blaming individuals rather than on understanding the wider context. One problem with this kind of approach is that it fails fully to make the most of any underlying opportunities to learn and develop. It can also mean that there is limited exploration of alternatives and a feeling on the part of the management team that they have been deprived of their authority or power to address the underlying problems. Moreover, when senior individuals are sacked this can be extremely disruptive to the business and its internal and external stakeholders.

Many of the above problems can be avoided if the leadership risks and issues relating to the investee business are explored systematically through the framework set out in this book. The following section introduces the four stages of the framework.

2.2   OVERVIEW OF THE STAGES OF THE FRAMEWORK

In highlighting the key considerations which need to be borne in mind at each stage of the framework, it is useful to use the four-quadrant model introduced in Chapter 1. As described earlier, it is important to remain aware of both the inner world and the outer world of the investee being assessed, as well as the inner and outer world of the investor and, critically, the way in which key issues in each of these four quadrants affect one another. See Figure 2.2.

2.2.1   Prepare Phase

In the preparation phase, the primary emphasis is on establishing the overall objectives of the assessment and identifying an efficient and effective means of achieving those objectives. From the investor's perspective, the 'outer' factors to consider will be around developing and communicating a clear and systematic approach. Particularly in cases where the investor is the primary driver of the assessment, it is very important that they are able to communicate a clear sense of the

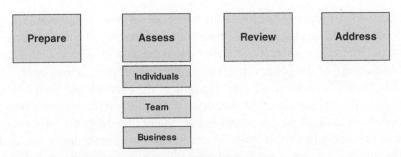

Figure 2.2   Management risk mapping framework

purpose of the exercise and rationale behind. It is also vital to pro-vide an overview of the process which will ensure that both participants and people in the wider businesses know what to expect. The investor needs to remain aware of the importance of being open and collaborative at this stage, and show themself willing to answer questions. This will minimise the perception of the assessment as a threat, and ideally will present the exercise as something which is supportive and constructive and set a positive tone. Inwardly, the investor also needs to remain vig-ilant to emotional factors which could impede proper and systematic planning of the exercise. A common temptation is to be impatient to get on with the review, and the consequence of this is that there is inadequate preparation, leading to a less than satisfactory result. It is also useful for the investor to remain alert to feelings stemming from the conditions which have given rise to the leadership risk assessment. For example, if a portfolio business has not been performing as well as expected and the leadership risk assessment is planned in order to investigate how to address this, it is possible that the investor will go into the exercise with feelings of disappointment and possibly even resentment. Remaining sensitive to such feelings will enable the investor to ensure that they do not impede the adequate planning of the exercise moving to the world of the investee management team in the preparatory phase. In the 'outer' world the preparation phase should help them to establish how much time they will need to make available for the exercise so that this can be properly scheduled. It is also useful for them to understand what other data they will have to make available. A further important aspect is the way in which the investee management team explains the process to the wider organisation. For example, if a 360-degree feedback review is planned, individuals from outside the senior management team will be required to participate in the process and it is important that everyone involved is properly briefed so that they know what to expect. A key 'outer'-world decision to be made here relates to who has ultimate ownership of the exercise. A fuller consideration of who should have 'ownership' of the process is given in the next chapter; it may be desirable for the investee team itself to conduct the exercise and then report back to the investor. In other situations, particularly if the review is being conducted as part of a pre-deal management due diligence process, it will inevitably be driven by the investor. In looking at the inner world of the investee management team during the preparation phase, it is useful to recognise whether there are any fears, doubts or anxieties about the process. Ideally, the investee management team should enter the process with a sense of positive anticipation, and a sense of reassurance that they are about to embark on an exercise which will help them and their business. Inadequate communication in the preparation phase can make this difficult, so that management feel instead self-conscious and anxious about the prospect of 'being tested'.

2.2.2   Assess Phase

Looking next at the assessment phase, the emphasis in the outer world of the investor is to ensure that data are gathered in a thorough and systematic fashion. If proper preparation has been done, the right topics and questions will have been identified and, if applicable, suitable psychometric instruments will have been selected. In the assess phase it is a matter of working through these to build a picture. Probably the biggest risk here is being too quick to attempt to interpret the data before it has all been gathered. Another risk is to rely on the preconceived solutions without fully considering the specifics of the situation. Beneath the surface, the inner world of the investor during the assess phase may be affected by scepticism about some of the tools and techniques which are being used. As we have discussed earlier, private equity investors generally have a preference for quantitative financial analysis and the leadership risk review forces them into the world of the nonquantifiable, which may be outside their comfort zone and can mean that they are reluctant to engage with the data being generated.

On the investee side, the 'outer' world factors to be sensitive to at this stage are around remaining authentic and being cooperative in providing the data which is requested. Therefore, they should be as open and patient as possible in answering questions and aim for candour and transparency. It is also important that they make time and give proper attention to the exercise – so, for example, they should resist the temptation to complete psychometric instruments or 360-degree feedback at a time when they are tired or likely to be distracted. On the other hand, it is also important that, while the senior management team are undergoing a leadership risk assessment, they do not let the exercise distract them from the day-to-day running of the business. On an 'inner' level the members of the investee management team should be aware of any feelings of suspicion or caution they may have about exposing perceived weaknesses and remain aware that the ultimate aim of the exercise is a positive and constructive one.

2.2.3 Review Phase

The emphasis during the review phase is on analysing the data gathered during the assessment in a systematic fashion, comparing and triangulating information gathered from different sources and exploring emerging themes arising at different levels. As themes and issues emerge they can then be linked back to the relevant elements of the context on the basis of which the review was planned. From the investor's point of view, the emphasis in the outer world is on reviewing the documentation in a systematic fashion and linking it back to business performance. The aim is to establish 'golden threads' which run through the outputs from the review and can be connected with particular business outcomes. It is important here to remain focused on risks and implications. If at all possible, it is probably best if the investor and the investee management team review the results together and the process of interpretation and exploration of the risks is one of joint collaboration. In any event it is important, if the assessment has been done by the investor, to avoid being too secretive. Development activities arising from the review will in any case largely need to be undertaken on the part of the investee management team, so at some stage or other they need to be made aware of the results. As issues emerge in the review phase it is important to prioritise them on the basis of the potential impact they may have on the business and the time frame within which they may materialise. During the review phase, aspects of the investor's 'inner' world which deserve attention may include a tendency to 'blame' members of the management team for poor business performance and use the data from the assessments to build a case against them. It is very important that the review is conducted in an objective and impartial manner and, as far as possible, themes and issues should be depersonalised. On a deeper level, the investor may be confronted with a growing awareness that some factors influencing poor business performance could actually be their fault. For example, they may come to realise that more investigation should have been done before the deal was completed and that issues emerging from the review were actually evident all along. From the investee management team's perspective, the review phase represents an opportunity to show an open and collaborative attitude. If the review has been conducted by the investor, there may be questions about how much access they have to the findings. As mentioned above, it is probably best if the review is conducted jointly. If, on the other hand, the investee management team have taken the lead in conducting the review, they will be thinking about how best to present the results. Aspects of the 'inner' world of the investee management team during the review phases centre around understanding and awareness. There will be a natural tendency to take any negative feedback personally and possibly react emotionally. Such emotional reactions can make it difficult to 'process' the messages objectively and use the insights arising from the review in a constructive way for the good of the business. There can also be a tendency to dwell unduly on the negative messages and ignore the positive ones. It is important during the review phase that the investee management team who have undergone the assessment have sufficient time and space to digest and process the feedback.

2.2.4   Address Phase

During the address phase the findings of the review are translated into development plans which should then be implemented over time. It is vital that this is not seen as the end but rather the beginning of a new developmental phase. The art of addressing salient issues effectively is to identify pragmatic and creative solutions and approaches which therefore lead to manifest benefits within the business. Key aspects to bear in mind at this stage include making clear distinctions between what can and cannot be changed and identifying strategies for keeping the development agenda alive. In the 'outer' world of the investor the address phase will involve setting targets and measures for planned developments. It is important that the investor and investee management team remain reasonably flexible to allow for fine-tuning of development plans in the light of further experience. At this stage the investor may conclude that some significant business issues do not in fact stem from leadership risks to the extent that they had previously assumed. In this case it may be necessary to conduct further investigation to identify other causes. It may also be necessary to revise business plans and projections. Tensions may arise in the investor's 'inner' world during the address phase because of their impatience to find solutions to the problems which have been identified. In planning how best to address the findings of the review, it is important that decisions are not rushed. Grave errors can be made at this phase – for example, if the investor makes a snap decision to fire someone from the investee management team rather than give adequate consideration to whether there was an option of developing that individual. Moreover, they may not fully think through the costs and consequences of making such a significant change in the senior team. During the address phase all parties should be realistic about whether they can address the issues identified themselves or whether they require support from a third party (such as an executive coach). From the investee management team's perspective, the emphasis during the address phase is on clearly identifying expectations, outcomes and timings for development and building realistic and focused personal and team development plans. Consideration should also be given to the communication which they may have to take place in the wider organisation and how best to manage this. As mentioned previously, during the development planning phase, there needs to be some flexibility to allow for further fine-tuning. Members of the investee management team should be careful during this phase to remain alert to an inner tendency to be possibly overconfident with regard to their development plans. It is important for them to find ways to tap into their inner motivation and to find that part of themselves that will give them the inner momentum to see their development plans through to fruition. It is also important to recognise that the chances of successfully realising their development plans will be maximised if members of the management team are mutually cooperative and supportive to one another and are not afraid to acknowledge when and where they may need help and support.

Having looked at the four phases of the framework, in subsequent chapters we will now unpack these in greater detail – starting with the prepare phase in the next chapter. At the start of each of the following chapters we will present a short summary of the key risks which the tools and techniques in that chapter will help to address.

2.3 SUMMARY

- Given the high level of complexity associated with leadership risk, it is not feasible to envisage a single system which could address this.

Instead, the leadership risk mapping framework integrates multiple views.

- The framework looks at multiple levels of leadership – individual, team and organisation.
- The framework also gathers data from multiple perspectives including self, others and data on the context.
- The framework follows a systematic, four-stage process: prepare, assess, review, address.
- The systematic process helps to avoid making rash interventions when leadership issues arise.
- In each of the four stages of the framework, the four quadrants of awareness can be used to ensure a robust and thorough approach to the mapping and management of leadership risk.

3

Planning and Preparation

Risks associated with the planning and preparation phase include:

- The approach is not sufficiently tailored to the specific context of the business.
- The review does not yield results which are sufficiently relevant.
- Past mistakes (in how to approach leadership assessment) are repeated.
- The review is conducted in a way which sours the relationship between the investor and investee management team.
- Time, energy and other resources are not used efficiently.
- The review does not lead to lasting benefits to the business and underlying issues and problems go unaddressed.

3.1 INTRODUCTION

The planning and preparation phase is probably the most critical element of the leadership risk mapping process. The benefits of discipline and focus which come from having a structured framework, as described in Chapter 2, are all rooted in a process of proper planning and preparation. Making a sufficient investment of time and energy during the planning phase will help to maximise the value of the overall process. Proper preparation helps to establish transparency in a way which ensures that everybody involved is clear about what is going to be done and why, and this in turn helps to maintain and build trust. Planning also helps to ensure that focus is maintained on the business and business outcomes, and establishes logical links between the approach selected and the outputs which are sought. Careful preparation also helps to ensure that the traps and pitfalls associated with the complex process of leadership risk mapping are avoided, and to ensure that awareness is raised in the right areas in a constructive, supportive and nonjudgemental manner. Having a clear roadmap of the process will mean that the reviewer is less likely to jump to false conclusions or make wrong assumptions.

Some of the key questions that must be addressed in the planning phase include the following:

- What is the overall purpose of this review?
- If it goes as well as it possibly can, what will the outputs be and where will we be at the end of the process?
- To achieve the objectives of the process, who needs to do what and when?
- Will third parties need to be involved and, if so, who, when and how?
- Who will have overall ownership of the process?
- How can we ensure that the process yields maximum benefits whilst causing minimum disruption to the ongoing business?

This chapter looks at how to establish a clear and focused plan for conducting a leadership risk assessment. We begin the chapter by working through each of the four quadrants of awareness introduced previously. For each of the four quadrants we describe the themes and issues which need to be borne in mind during the planning phase and highlight the key questions to be considered. The answers to these questions can then be used to formulate the overall plan, and we suggest a structure which can be used for this. Finally, we will also consider the critical importance of adequate communication and, in light of this, set out the components of a suitable communication plan.

3.2   PLANNING THROUGH THE FOUR QUADRANTS OF AWARENESS

As mentioned in the previous chapter, given the complexities and sensitivities associated with leadership risk mapping, it is important for the investor to consider both the visible, outer perspective of the investee leadership team and also to remain vigilant to the impact of what may be happening below the surface at a deeper, unspoken level. We also highlighted the importance of the investor considering their own impact on the process, again both from an outer and inner perspective. The resulting four quadrants of awareness provide a useful structure through which the relevant questions which need to be considered during the planning phase can be explored.

3.2.1   The Outer Perspective of the Investee

The natural starting point when planning a leadership risk assessment is the outer perspective of the investee. One of the most fundamental factors influencing the planning of a leadership risk assessment is the point in the lifecycle of the investment at which the review will be taking place. The most obvious distinction here is whether the review is to take place before the transaction, in which case it will effectively be a kind of management due diligence review or whether the leadership risk assessment is to be conducted once the business has become part of the investor's portfolio. Typical scenarios would include the following:

- If the review is conducted shortly after acquisition, the overall purpose of the review will be to ensure that the leadership team get off to the best possible start with a clear and focused development agenda and a feeling of being reassured and supported by the investor.
- Where the review takes place some time after acquisition (possibly 12 to 18 months), the purpose and therefore the plan may be different. It could be, for example, that doubts have emerged as to whether there is really a shared vision for the business between investor and investee management team or whether there is full agreement about the best strategy.
- It could also be that results have not been as good as expected and that the review is intended to explore the reasons for this and identify means of addressing underlying problems.
- A further scenario for an ongoing portfolio review could be that there is a perception on the part of the investor and/or the investee management team that, although business results are satisfactory, there is remaining scope to take the business 'to the next level' and the aim is to decide how best to achieve this.
- It may also be that the review is conducted closer to the expected exit point. Here, the purpose of the review may be to identify what needs to be done in order to ensure that business results are as strong as possible in the run-up to exit. It may also be useful to raise awareness of how the management team either individually or collectively may be perceived by a possible future investor.

The above represent a few of many possible scenarios which could prompt a leadership risk assessment. The important thing to consider is that each different scenario implies different outcomes and objectives and that different outcomes and objectives will have implications for the choice of approach and therefore a different plan. Making sure that proper consideration is given in this area helps to mitigate the risk that an overly standardised approach is used which could lead to irrelevant results, meaning that important issues are overlooked. General questions which need to be considered then are:

- What is the ultimate purpose of the review?
- What are the key questions which the review has to answer?

Once the purpose of the review has been clarified, the plan then needs to address what the scope will be. The framework is based around the idea of assessing leadership risk on several dimensions and, for each of these dimensions, considering multiple perspectives. Depending on the scenario and the goal of the review, each level of analysis may take on a different emphasis. In most cases, the individual level of analysis will attract most attention and it is hard to envisage a review of this nature being conducted without at least some assessment of the individual members of the leadership team. Whether or not team-level or business-level assessment is conducted, and in what depth this is done, will vary. A significant factor to consider here is the degree of access which the investor will have to the management team. If the review is being conducted as part of a management due diligence exercise before the transaction is completed, there may be limited access to the management team and also limited time available in which to conduct the review. Moreover, if the review is being done pre-deal, it is very unlikely that some techniques (for example, 360-degree or multi-rater feedback) will be feasible – the following chapters provide much greater detail on how to decide the best approach for assessing at different levels. For the purpose of the current chapter, the important point to bear in mind is that once the purpose, scope and approach have been decided, this should then be clearly documented in a detailed plan for the review, including a timetable.

It may be tempting to conclude that consideration of the factors described above will provide a sufficient basis for establishing a comprehensive project plan; however, both of these documents also need to reflect relevant issues from the three other quadrants of awareness, as will be described below.

3.2.2   The Outer Perspective of the Investor

As with other stages of the leadership risk mapping framework, the tendency is for the investor to focus most attention on the outer perspective of the investee team. However, there are also a number of factors relating to the investor themself which can usefully be borne in mind. One element here is to consider what other information is available to the investor and the implications of this for the leadership risk review. If the review is being conducted before the deal, as part of management due diligence, it is likely that by the time the review takes place, a good deal of other, 'harder' data will be available. Management due diligence is often conducted after financial and strategic due diligence reviews have taken place, and both of these can yield important pointers as to where management due diligence should focus. As we will explain in more detail in later chapters, it is important for the investor to explore critically the business case for the investment from a leadership perspective. The business case for the investment in the strategic plan can be seen as representing an, albeit rather abstract, roadmap of how value will be created in the investment. During the planning and preparation phase it is useful for the investor to walk through this plan and consider its key milestones in terms of the principal decisions and main challenges it implies for the leadership team. One useful way to think about this is to consider the critical path to exit from a behavioural or leadership perspective. A point of reference here can be the 'J curve'. The J curve is often used to illustrate the pattern of returns in private equity portfolios over time, and the performance of individual portfolio businesses can also follow a similar pattern. Given private equity investors' familiarity with this pattern, it may be helpful to frame some of the key leadership challenges which the business will face at different points on its journey to exit.

Figure 3.1 indicates how different phases in the development of the investee business correspond to different leadership challenges and hence different risks.

Anticipating these challenges and thinking about how to address them will increase the likelihood of success. As an illustration, the leadership challenges at each of the highlighted stages of the business above could include the following.

At **Stage 1** the deal has only just taken place and the key leadership challenges relate to getting the business off to the best possible start in the post-deal phase. It could be that, for the previous few months, considerable time and energy were expended by the management team in negotiating the deal. Some members of the management team may be suffering from deal fatigue. However, from this point on the focus is on translating the strategic plan into reality. At this very early stage in the lifecycle of the investment, a further leadership challenge stems from the need to manage some of the changes which may have arisen at the time of the deal. In particular, it is important for the management team to begin to

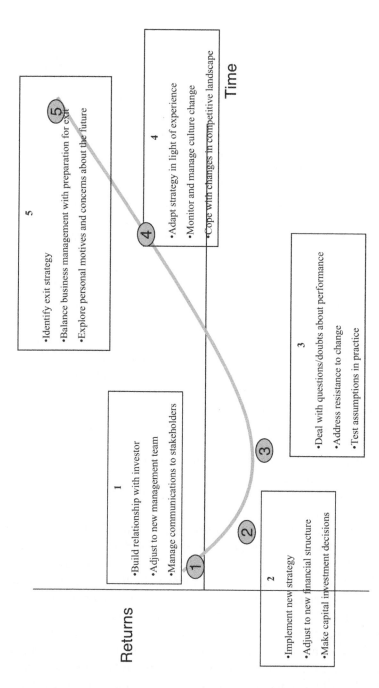

Figure 3.1 Leadership challenges through the J-curve

Returns

Time

1
•Build relationship with investor
•Adjust to new management team
•Manage communications to stakeholders

2
•Implement new strategy
•Adjust to new financial structure
•Make capital investment decisions

3
•Deal with questions/doubts about performance
•Address resistance to change
•Test assumptions in practice

4
•Adapt strategy in light of experience
•Monitor and manage culture change
•Cope with changes in competitive landscape

5
•Identify exit strategy
•Balance business management with preparation for exit
•Explore personal motives and concerns about the future

forge an effective working relationship with the private equity investor. It could also be that new members have joined the management team or previous members have left (for example, a founder of the business may have sold their stake as part of the deal). A number of key stakeholders in the business – including employees, customers and suppliers – will also be aware of the deal and careful consideration needs to be given to the messages which need to be communicated to these groups and how best to do this.

At **Stage 2** the business will be up and running and the key leadership challenges will relate to working through some of the main strategic milestones. At this stage, the full implications of the new financial structure of the business will be felt and the leadership team will have a clearer sense of what the new investor's involvement feels like in practice. It is likely that the business will have access to more capital but will be carrying more debt, and the leadership team may have to recalibrate their perspective and become accustomed to making business decisions on a much bigger scale than they have done previously.

By **Stage 3** there will be a much clearer sense of how well the strategy is working and to what extent the assumptions made at the time of the deal were accurate. By this stage there may have been unforeseen developments in the market or the wider economy, and the leadership team will face the challenge of how to react. The full extent of internal reactions to change initiatives will also be felt at this point, so a further leadership challenge could relate to how best to react to resistance to change within the business. On an inner level, some members of the management team may feel that the optimism that they felt at the time of the deal has started to falter. The business may not be performing as well as expected, and the leadership team will have to cope with any doubts they feel or which they sense are coming from the investor.

By **Stage 4**, the business feels to be on track and the key leadership challenge is around maintaining momentum and fine-tuning the strategy in light of experience. At this stage, competitors will have a much clearer view of the strategy being followed and may have launched reactive strategies of their own, so it is critical that the leadership are sensitive to changes in the competitive landscape. There may still be residual currents of resistance to change on a cultural level at this stage, so a further leadership challenge is noticing and engaging with these.

By **Stage 5**, the end of this particular business cycle is in sight. One of the key leadership challenges at this stage is for leaders to identify and evaluate the options which exist for exit whilst still preserving sufficient energy and attention for them to run the business successfully. On a more personal level, at this stage members of the management team may also be reflecting on whether their future lies with the business in its next phase or elsewhere and, if so, how this can be negotiated so as not to impair the exit.

The plan will make various assumptions and project various scenarios and it is useful to consider what each of these implies for the leadership team of the business. If the deal is to be conducted on an existing portfolio investment, it is important that the investor revisits some of the projections and assumptions which were made at the time of the original investment as these will give important clues as to which dimensions of leadership will be important and, therefore, need to be assessed. It is possible, and in many cases likely, that certain assumptions made at the time of investment have subsequently proved to be inaccurate. As well as unexpected changes within the business, it is possible that there will have been unexpected developments in the market and possibly in the wider economy, and each of these may imply a different emphasis in terms of which skills and abilities will be most important to assess. It is therefore important that one aspect of the investor's own 'outer' world for them to reflect on during the planning and preparation phase is their existing map and basis for understanding the investee business.

Another important factor for the investor to consider is how well their existing process for assessing leadership and leadership risk actually works. Given the reduced emphasis and lower priority which is often given to leadership assessment as compared with financial and strategic analysis, it is possible that investors evolve and become comfortable with a standard approach to leadership assessment which is rarely challenged or critically reviewed. A useful step in the preparation phase, which can be conducted long before a specific leadership review is foreseen, is for the investor to stand back and critically explore what can be learned from previous management assessments which have been conducted. Significant value can be derived from such an exercise as it is possible to evaluate the process used for the review and the outputs it produced in terms of the subsequent performance of the leadership team and the business which they were leading. A reflective review of this kind will usually involve an examination of the relevant documentation (leadership assessment reports and performance data from the business) as a starting point for discussing questions such as those listed below:

- What were the key findings of the review and how did these subsequently inform our management of the investment?

- What were the most and least useful parts of the process?
- In what ways did the review and its findings help to anticipate and mitigate risks and problems?
- What feedback did we get on the process from the management team(s) that were assessed?
- What, if any, impact did the review have on the relationship with the leadership team?
- Thinking back to how the business developed after the review and how the leadership team performed, what else could we, or should we, have explored as part of the assessment?
- What assumptions did we make in planning the assessment and how accurate were these?

A final, potentially significant, consideration is who should have 'ownership' of the leadership mapping review. The ultimate purpose of the review is to identify and mitigate leadership risks so as to ensure that the business performs as well as possible. This outcome is in the interests of both the investor and the investee. There may be a natural tendency on the part of the investor that the review is something they should 'do' or 'have done' *to* the investee business. Whilst this will almost certainly be the case if the review is done as part of pre-deal due diligence, it should not necessarily be assumed that the investor must be the driver of the process if it is done on an existing portfolio business. There is an argument that the process might arrive at an even clearer, richer view if the investee management team themselves 'own' the process and then share the results with the investor. Such an approach reinforces the point that the ultimate performance of the investee business rests in the hands of its senior management team. This approach further mitigates the risk of alienating the management team by making them feel they are having something done to them, over which they have no control.

The outer world of the investor can therefore provide valuable insights during the planning phase, both in terms of deciding how other available data can usefully influence the scope and focus of the leadership risk assessment and by highlighting lessons which can be learned from past experience. Having considered the outer perspective of both the investee business and the investor, we can now look at the inner dimensions of both parties and see how insights here can also be of benefit during the planning phase.

3.2.3   The Inner World of the Investee Management Team

The common concern among investors considering leadership assessment, particularly as part of pre-deal management due diligence, is that the process should not impair the fledgling relationship between the investor and the investee management team. Careful planning of how to structure the approach and how to communicate it can help significantly, not only in mitigating the risk of souring the relationship with the investee team, but also in highlighting ways in which the leadership risk assessment can actually be used to strengthen that relationship. Further consideration of this dimension is facilitated if the investor is able actively to put themselves in the shoes of the investee team. As the plan is being developed, the investor should constantly ask what it would feel like to be on the receiving end of such a process and what fears and concerns it may trigger on the part of the investee management team. Careful and comprehensive communication can be of significant benefit here. Ensuring that the team being assessed fully understand what is going to be done and why it is very important. As far as possible the approach should be planned so as to ensure that, rather than feeling they are being 'tested', the investee team come to view the process as supportive and ultimately in everyone's best interest as it will maximise the chances of success in the business. Elements of the communication to the investee management team should provide a clear picture of:

- The overall process – overall aims and approach.
- The timing of the process and its constituent elements – what will be done and when.
- How much time each member of the team will have to set aside.
- Who will be conducting the review – if a third party is involved, the name of the organisation and the individuals doing the assessment.
- What members of the management team will experience.
- What they should do if they have any questions – names and contact details.
- The feedback process – when they will receive feedback and from whom.
- What the outcomes of the assessment will be, for example, greater understanding of themselves which can be used to create a development plan.

Underlying the communication should be the message that the review is constructive and will ultimately provide the individuals and the team as a whole with useful support for their ongoing development.

Careful planning will also help to ensure that the investee team will not experience unnecessary stress and frustration, which can be prompted by a leadership review process which takes too long and causes disruption to the business. A further inner aspect of the investee management team which is important to bear in mind is the level of energy they will have available to invest in the process. If, for example, the leadership risk assessment is to be conducted towards the end of the due diligence process in the final weeks before the deal takes place, it is important to bear in mind that by this stage the leadership team are likely to be extremely tired, having just lived through several months of working through the deal negotiations whilst still trying to manage the business. In light of this, serious consideration should be given to maybe changing the timing of the review and postponing it until after the deal has taken place, at which stage the mood and energy levels of the management team are likely to be quite different. As well as the inner dimension of the investee team, it is also important during the planning phase that the investor maintains awareness of what will be going on in their own inner world, and this is described further in the following section.

3.2.4   The Inner World of the Investor

To maximise the opportunity of conducting a thorough and useful leadership risk assessment, it is important for the investor to reflect on any deeper, unspoken issues on their part which could impair the process. Despite the logical case for performing a thorough leadership risk assessment, there may be deeper, less rational reasons why an investor may be tempted to avoid or limit the scope of a leadership review.

One example of this, which can manifest in the pre-deal phase, is the phenomenon of deal momentum. Anyone who has worked in private equity will know what it is like to become attached to a deal on an emotional level. Experienced investors will have witnessed, or experienced for themselves, the phenomenon of deal momentum, where so much time and energy are invested in a deal that objectivity is lost and potentially negative information about the investment is rejected. This problem is compounded because the essence of the private equity investor's job is to 'do deals'.

In the pre-deal phase there is also a general tendency for all parties to focus on the upside. It is obvious that the seller has a big incentive to focus purely on the upside and make the case for the deal. Yet in some cases the buyer will also fall prey to focusing exclusively on the positive and neglecting any potential downsides to the deal. The investor will be under pressure to invest significant amounts of money, along with the funds of backers. There is an opportunity cost to not investing money. If the private equity fund cannot show a good track record of choosing and investing in winning businesses, its reputation may suffer, and it will face challenges trying to attract limited partners in the future.

It is important not to underestimate the power of deal momentum. Once the due diligence process has been set in motion, or even before, momentum will build to increasing levels as the deal is 'talked up' and more resources are devoted to evaluating it. Hopes and expectations are raised, and individuals may come to identify more and more strongly with the prospective deal. Issues such as reputation, ego and pride may come into play as well. It is not hard to see how the whole process can become like a runaway train. Even if individuals develop creeping doubts as to the deal's viability, as it consumes more time and money, it may become more difficult to call a halt to the process.

Within the context of a potential private equity investment, there may be strong and unspoken pressure to 'go with the flow' and support the deal even in the face of indications that the deal is not worth pursuing. There is always a risk that investors override their reservations about a potential deal or member of a management team, sometimes based on gut feel, only to have their doubts borne out later. Within the context of the current chapter, it is important for investors to remain vigilant to the phenomena of deal momentum, as these are tendencies which may limit their willingness to fully explore management risk. This risk is perhaps more pronounced in relation to management risk at a business level, where potential obstacles to success exist within the business as a whole and cannot be attributed to or 'blamed' on key individuals.

A further factor stemming from the 'inner' world of the investor, which could prompt resistance to some leadership risk mapping techniques, is their general attachment to the financial paradigm and an innate scepticism to qualitative approaches. It may be, for example, that private equity investors have an innate bias against, or even hatred of, psychological approaches to assessment which could lead them to discount such techniques.

It can therefore be seen that the four quadrants model can usefully be employed in the preparation stage in order to maximise the chances that the resulting plan will be as effective as possible.

3.2.5   Output

Once the factors described above have been fully considered, it should be possible to set out a written plan for the review. A typical plan would include the following elements:

Elements of the plan	Comments
Areas of emphasis	A description of the key elements of the strategy which have significant leadership implications. Description of key points to probe under each of the areas: individual, team and group.
Overall timetable	A detailed description of each stage of the process, how long it will take, when it will be done and by whom. A typical running order would be: • Prepare briefing and other communication materials • Brief participants • Liaise with third-party providers • Set up questionnaires • Conduct interviews • Set a deadline for the gathering of all data • Review data • Schedule feedback discussions with participants • Set a deadline for submission of personal development plans • Review development plans • Implement development plans • Conduct ongoing review.
Points of sensitivity	Details of any concerns or hypotheses or any other issues which require probing or confirmation that stem from the investor's gut feel.
Third-party providers	Contact details of any third parties who will be assisting with the assessment, including when they will be involved, who the key contact is.
Participants	Names and full contact details and role descriptions for all participants; description of any teams which will be assessed and their members.

3.3   SUMMARY

• The planning and preparation phase is probably the most critical stage in the process.
• The four quadrants of awareness provide a useful structure around which to manage the planning.
• The context surrounding the leadership risk mapping exercise is significant and a number of scenarios are possible.

- For any given scenario the most important thing is to have a clear sense of the questions which the review has to answer.
- Another important part of the preparation is for the investor to consider fully the other information which they have available.
- The investor should plan the review using 'harder' data from strategic and financial due diligence.
- It is also important for the investor to reflect carefully on the leadership agenda, depending on where the business is in its lifecycle.
- Reflecting on what did and did not go well in previous leadership assessments and learning from these is a useful discipline.
- Another key decision in the planning phase is who should have overall ownership of the process.
- It is important to remain aware of any inner fears and concerns that the investee management team may have. Clear and comprehensive communication can help to alleviate these.
- When thinking about the best time to conduct the review, it is also important to recognise how much time and energy the investee team will have for the process.
- If the review is done as part of due diligence, the investor should guard against deal momentum as this may tempt them to limit or avoid the leadership assessment.
- The investor should also challenge any tendency they may feel to discount information which is not expressed in financial terms.

4

Deciding What to Assess at an Individual Level

Risks associated with the decision of what to assess at an individual level include:

- The assessment is based on too narrow a range of characteristics so that key aspects are overlooked.
- The profile of leadership effectiveness on which the assessment is based is either too simplistic or too elaborate to be workable.
- Key individuals are only looked at from one dimension.
- Insufficient planning is done on what to assess so that the assessment process is flawed.
- The assessment looks at individuals purely in terms of strengths and weaknesses so derailment risks are overlooked.

4.1 INTRODUCTION

Assessment at an individual level lies at the very heart of the leadership risk mapping framework. The potential of the business to succeed or fail lies to a great degree within the senior individuals whose job it is to lead it. As we will see in the following chapters, assessment at the other organisational levels (team and business levels) also builds on what emerges at an individual level. However, assessment at the individual level is far from straightforward. Compared with the team and business levels of assessment, it is likely that the assessment of individuals is an area which the investor already has the clearest view in terms of what needs to be assessed and how the assessment should be conducted. However, this carries with it the risk that a predefined and formulaic approach is followed which is not sufficiently linked to the specifics of the business in question. Moreover, the 'gut feel' of the investor is likely to be strongest at the level of key individuals, and whilst this can be an extremely useful guide and act as a prompt as to which aspects to probe and assess in detail, it may also act as a distraction and tempt the investor to short-circuit the assessment process. Assessment at this level is also complex because the aspects of key individuals which need to be explored are not clear cut. As we will discuss in detail below, it is important not to oversimplify when exploring the characteristics which determine the effectiveness of senior leaders and so the ultimate success of the business. The possession of certain skills and knowledge is no guarantee that these will be applied effectively, and some 'leadership strengths' can be of benefit in some situations but actively harmful in others.

At a simple level the assessment of senior individuals needs to address two core questions:

- 'Can they do it?'
- 'Will they do it?'

These two questions can be related back to the inner game formula that was introduced earlier. The question of 'Can they do it?' relates to the potential latent within the key individuals and the question 'Will they do it?' relates to the extent to which other factors may come to interfere with, and ultimately affect, performance. In line with the key principles underpinning the leadership risk mapping framework, the complex decision of what to assess on an individual level is addressed by exploring it from a number of perspectives. We suggest that to build a rich and rounded picture of the key individuals being assessed it is necessary to raise awareness of three distinct perspectives:

- Skills and competencies – the extent to which they exhibit certain key behaviours and skills which impact the business.
- Personality traits – their inner psychological preferences, the implications of these and the impact which they have.
- Drivers and motivators – their core values and what it is they strive to achieve or avoid.

Each of these dimensions is discussed below. For each dimension we have provided an explanation of what it relates to and why it is important from a leadership risk perspective. We have also shown how the four quadrants of awareness can be used to prompt the kind of questions which are useful to consider when planning what to assess. For each dimension we have also given a brief indication of some of the general aspects which are often relevant when assessing the leaders of private equity-backed businesses. We then set out a number of the general characteristics shared by some of the most successful private equity-backed chief executives. Following the description of the individual dimensions to be explored during individual-level assessment, we then set out an illustration of how particular points of emphasis across these dimensions may change depending on the specific business scenario and strategy. This illustrates the critical importance of taking sufficient account of context when deciding what to assess.

4.2   LEADERSHIP COMPETENCIES

Competencies are simply a way of defining the behaviours and skills that are likely to predict effectiveness – in this context, in senior leadership positions. In relation to the 'inner game' equation introduced previously, understanding an individual's level on the core competencies relevant to the business is helpful in gauging their potential to perform and so helps to provide an answer to the question 'Can they do it?' In the context of leadership risk mapping, part of the task of the investor is to understand the skills that leaders will require to succeed in the venture, and competency theory is one way to describe these. It has often been argued that the best predictor of future performance is past performance, and competencies provide a framework for mapping and dissecting past performance. Of the three dimensions discussed in this chapter, competencies are arguably the most accessible as they deal with what is observable and the links with performance are more explicit.

The use of competencies can be very helpful within the context of the senior executive in assessment. In order to develop the competency framework it is necessary to reflect carefully on the behaviours which bring the best outcomes. Rather than talking merely of good and bad leadership performance, such frameworks encourage reflection and exploration of what 'good' looks like. Competency frameworks also help to establish an objective basis for evaluating performance, and make it possible to compare the performance of different individuals within a leadership population on a consistent basis. As a result, competency frameworks often form the basis of performance management systems within the organisations and are used extensively as a development planning tool. With respect to leadership risk mapping, it can also be extremely useful to establish a kind of competency framework as a means of clarifying the skills and behaviours which the senior leaders of the investee business will need in order to succeed. However, before examining what a competency framework for private equity-backed leaders might look like, it is important to highlight some of the inherent limitations of this approach.

Firstly, the creation of competency frameworks involves an inevitable process of simplification. Although it is very useful to examine the links between behaviour and business success and failure, it is important to remember that the outcomes ultimately achieved are the result of many factors, only one of which is leadership behaviour. As discussed at the beginning of this book, the causal chain of value creation and destruction is complex and opaque and no list of leadership behaviours, however long and detailed, could come close to fully accounting for this. Another problem with competency frameworks is that they encourage the view that there are certain 'universal' leadership behaviours which drive success. As a result, the significance of context may be overlooked, leading to a view that the same set of skills and behaviours can be guaranteed across a variety of businesses, which is unlikely to be the case. A final aspect of competency frameworks requiring caution when they are used as part of a leadership risk mapping exercise is the way in which they suggest that the demonstration of a competency and a resulting leadership effectiveness are related in a linear manner. This suggests that the more one exhibits or demonstrates a particular leadership skill, the better the results. However, there is empirical evidence which suggests that many leadership competencies have a 'shelf life' and that overuse of certain competencies can actually lead to derailment. Derailment refers to the situation in which a senior executive with a strong track record either plateaus or exits an organisation as a result of a misfit between his or her skill sets and the requirements of the job. As these high performers faced changing demands as they moved up within their organisations, some of the strengths that served them best became weaknesses, and weaknesses that had not mattered in the past became issues. The Center for Creative Leadership has conducted studies on derailment since the 1970s, first in the USA and then expanding its research to encompass a global population of senior managers.

Their research shows that the main causes of executive derailment fall into four areas:

- Problems with interpersonal relationships.
- Failure to meet business objectives.
- Failure to build and lead a team.
- Inability to change or adapt during a transition.

From a leadership risk assessment perspective, the notion of derailment has great significance as it suggests that certain apparent leadership strengths carry with them the seeds of problems to come. This emphasises the importance of thinking through the leadership agenda which lies ahead and how it might play out for a particular leader, given their preferred style, rather than simply extrapolating from the past and assuming that, because they have always been a 'good leader' previously, this is bound to continue.

Despite these limitations it is useful to draw upon the idea of leadership competencies when deciding what to assess as part of a leadership risk assessment.

Leadership risks relating to competencies include the following:

- The individual members of the senior team do not have the necessary skills to lead the business to a successful exit.
- Individual members of the management team overuse certain competencies.
- The skill sets of individual members of the senior management team do not fit the requirements of the business.
- There is insufficient understanding of the links between leadership behaviour and the desired business outcomes.

In deciding what to assess in the area of individual competencies, it is useful to use the four quadrants of awareness model as a means of prompting questions.

Investee's 'outer' perspective
- What is the leadership agenda through to exit and what leadership skills will be required to deliver this?
- Where are each of the individual team members in terms of their current level on each of the relevant competencies and where do they need to develop?
- How will the competencies required of senior leaders change over time?

Investor's 'outer' perspective
- Thinking of the most successful and effective leaders we have worked with in the past, what were the key competencies which they displayed and to what extent could they be relevant here?

Investee's 'inner' perspective
- What apparent strengths does the individual have which could cause problems in the future and lead to the risk of derailment?

Investor's 'inner' perspective
- Reflecting on 'gut feel', what sense do we have of the individual's stronger and weaker areas and how can we test our instincts?

Throughout the different stages of this framework we have stressed the importance of a context to emphasise that the specific and unique characteristics of any given investee business receive sufficient attention. As we will illustrate later, different strategies can imply very different sets of competencies. However, experience suggests that there are some leadership competencies which will serve senior leaders well across a number of contexts.

These include:

- Managing ambiguity – the ability to make effective judgements and decisions across a range of different scenarios, including situations where data is incomplete or ambiguous.
- Inspirational leadership – the ability to reassure and inspire individuals and teams lower down the organisation and encourage them to perform at their best, even when negotiating significant change and working under considerable pressure.
- Adaptability – the ability to manage a wide and varied workload and adapt to shifting priorities.
- Team building – the ability to build focused and effective teams and cultivate a sense of cooperation and team spirit.
- Interpersonal relationships – the ability to forge and cultivate effective relationships with a wide range of different people.
- Delivery – the ability to understand clearly and consistently meet the expectations of key stakeholders (e.g. customers, investors, etc.).

4.3 PSYCHOLOGICAL TRAITS

In contrast to leadership competencies, which are largely visible, demonstrable and, to at least some degree, learnable, psychological traits exist much more in the inner world of the individual. Psychological traits relate to the various elements of personality and, in particular, the individual's core psychological preferences. From a leadership risk mapping perspective, having an awareness of the psychological traits of senior leaders in the investor business can be extremely useful as a basis for raising awareness around issues such as how well their personality preferences match the leadership agenda they are required to deliver, in what ways they are similar to or different from other members of the management team or representatives of the investor organisation, and what the implications of this might be and how they are likely to negotiate the various challenges which may arise in their role.

As with competencies, a broad range of psychological traits and preferences have been identified over the years. As we will discuss further in the next chapter, a range of psychometric tools exist which highlight different aspects of personality. A delicate balance is to be struck when considering the psychological dimension of senior leaders as part of a leadership risk mapping exercise. On the one hand, it is important to consider this deeper dimension as it can enhance or interfere with the individual's ability to reach their potential and also has a direct impact on their behaviour as leaders in areas such as decision making, problem solving and dealing with others. On the other hand, it is important not to get lost in the wilderness of human psychology, about which an enormous body of knowledge and theory exists. Engaging with the psychological dimension can be especially unpalatable for some private equity investors, for whom the 'touchy feely' aspect of leadership is anathema.

A manageable starting point in understanding personality traits within the current context is to consider what are known as the 'Big Five' personality characteristics. Rather than reflecting a model or theory of human psychology, these are simply the five dimensions on which people differ from one another in terms of their psychological preferences. They are:

- **Extraversion** – the amount of energy directed outwards into the external environment and the need for external stimulation.
- **Openness** – the individual's receptivity to a range of external and internal sources of new information and new input.
- **Agreeableness** – the role a person adopts in relationships along a continuum from compassion to antagonism and the likelihood of a person taking on board, accepting and being influenced by the perspectives and concerns of others.
- **Conscientiousness** – the person's strength of purpose and drive towards goal accomplishment.
- **Neuroticism** – the intensity and frequency of negative emotions arising from negative beliefs about life in general, oneself and other people and the impact of this on emotional adjustment.

Leadership risks relating to psychological traits include the following:

- Dominant psychological traits impede performance because the individual has a fixed repertoire of reactions.
- Lack of awareness of core psychological preferences leads to blind spots and recurrent patterns of behaviour.
- Failure to appreciate the impact of core psychological preferences on others leads to interpersonal problems.
- Lack of understanding and appreciation of the different preferences of other members of the senior leadership team leads to conflict.

The four quadrants of awareness model can be used to prompt questions around psychological traits, as follows.

Investee's 'outer' perspective
- Given the leadership agenda, which psychological traits will be the most significant?
- For the most significant psychological traits identified, what are the preferences of the individual leaders?
- What impact do the psychological characteristics of members of the management team have on others?

Investor's 'outer' perspective
- Thinking of the most successful and effective leaders we have worked with in the past, what were the key aspects of their character which made them effective and to what extent could they be relevant here?
- From past experience, which aspects of the personal psychology of individual leaders have caused problems and is this something we should look out for in the future?

Investee's 'inner' perspective
- To what extent are individual leaders aware of their psychological preferences?
- How do the traits and psychological characteristics of members of the management team, combined with their skills and competencies, affect performance?

Investor's 'inner' perspective
- Is there a risk that we may discount or avoid looking at the psychological dimension because this is not our preferred mode of looking at the world?

- How could our own psychological traits impact the leadership risk assessment process?
- Does 'gut feel' suggest there are any areas of the leader's individual psychology which require exploration?

As with competencies, great care should be taken when looking for 'universal' characteristics associated with leadership effectiveness across different contexts. However, successful leaders of private equity-backed businesses often share the following traits on four of the 'Big Five' described above:

- **On the Extraversion Scale** – a preference for taking control and strong appetite for being busy and moving at a fast pace.
- **On the Agreeableness Scale** – a preference for making rational, tough-minded decisions.
- **On the Conscientiousness Scale** – a highly goal-oriented style with a high level of inner determination.
- **On the Neuroticism Scale** – a high degree of emotional resilience and a low level of vulnerability to stress.

4.4 MOTIVATION

The remaining dimension to be considered when planning what to assess at an individual level relates to the inner drives and motivations of the leaders. These are the factors which are important for them personally – what they want to achieve and what they want to avoid. Although some drivers and motivators remain constant, others may change significantly over the course of an individual's career. The fact that personal motivations are not constant and may not even be clear to the individual concerned, yet still have the potential to impact choices, decisions and behaviour, means that they deserve careful consideration within the context of leadership risk mapping. During difficult times, which will almost inevitably arise on the journey to exit, having clear motivations and goals can have a positive impact in helping leaders to persevere. However, a lack of drive and clear sense of what engagement and sacrifice means for the leader may make them more likely to give up.

There is a common assumption in private equity that financial incentive is a significant motivating factor. This resonates with much of classical economic theory which is also predicated on assumptions about human decisions and human behaviour being driven by a desire to maximise financial gain. However, the motivations of senior leaders are worth exploring in further depth than this. It can be argued that, even if money is a motivating factor, this cannot necessarily be seen as an end in itself so it is worth exploring the particular meaning money has for the individual.

Individuals can be motivated by a wide variety of factors. They may be driven by a desire to move towards or achieve certain things and they may also be motivated by a need to avoid something. Different motivations take on different significance at different times and in different situations and they interact with personality traits and the skills and competencies which the individual has. Whilst the range of possible subjective motivations is almost infinite, beyond the basic requisites for survival (food, clothing, shelter, etc.), they usually fall into one of the following categories:

- *Security* – the ability to provide for oneself and one's family and have a sufficient buffer against unforeseen events.
- *Order* – the desire to have a degree of structure and predictability in one's life.
- *Affiliation* – the drive to have close, meaningful relationships with others.
- *Achievement* – the desire to fulfil one's potential and reach goals.
- *Approval* – the need to be recognised and respected by others.
- *Power* – the desire to exert control over one's surroundings or other people.
- *Autonomy* – the desire to be and feel in control of one's fate and not be controlled by others.
- *Comfort* – the need for enjoyment and gratification.

It can be seen from the above list that some motivations run counter to others, so it is not possible to aim for all of these at the same time. It should also be noted that human nature is such that, as one desire or motivation is satisfied, others will almost certainly emerge. Human motivation is therefore a cryptic and dynamic dimension of leadership.

Leadership risks relating to motivation include the following:

- The deeper motivations of investee leaders and the investor are not closely enough aligned.
- The motivations of individual leaders cause them to act in a way which is counter to the interests of the business.
- The motivations of leaders change during the lifecycle of the investment.
- Different members of the leadership team are driven by different motivations, which leads to conflict.

Questions to ask in the area of personal motivation include the following.

Investee's 'outer' perspective
- What are the key values and motivations of individual members of the management team?
- How have their motivations changed over time?
- What are they striving to achieve and avoid?
- How are the individual's motivations likely to change in the future?

Investor's 'outer' perspective
- Are there any differences between the motivations of the investor and the investee?
- What are the implications of any differences which may exist between the motivations of the management team and those of the investor?

Investee's 'inner' perspective
- How might the individuals' motivations interact with their psychological characteristics and competencies as a leader?
- Do any deeper motivations exist which the individual leader may be uncomfortable to discuss?
- How self-aware is the individual leader – have they really thought through their motivations and the implications of these?

Investor's 'inner' perspective
- Does the investor's 'gut feel' prompt any instinctive doubts about the degree and direction of the investee leader's motivation?

Some factors which it is useful to consider in relation to the motivation of the leaders of private equity-backed business are:

- Success (unsurprisingly) is often associated with individuals who have a high level of ambition and a need to achieve.
- Where the need for an adequate home life balance emerges, this can cause tension. This can arise if the individual begins a family during the lifecycle of the investment.
- The incentive to earn more may decline if leaders have completed several successful deals and they become more secure, but this may be replaced by a desire to apply the knowledge they have gained.
- Individuals who are motivated by a high level of structure and security will often struggle in private equity-backed businesses given the high levels of risk and the constant change.

4.5   SOME COMMON CHARACTERISTICS OF SUCCESSFUL PRIVATE EQUITY-BACKED CHIEF EXECUTIVES

The framework, around which this book is based, places a heavy emphasis on the importance of context. In identifying the appropriate areas to assess, we argue that it is critically important to take proper account of the challenges associated with the specific business in question rather than trying to base the assessment on a universal model of leadership effectiveness. We will illustrate the ways in which business context can influence what to assess at an individual level in the following section. Before doing this, it is useful to highlight some of the small number of characteristics which are present more often than not in the most effective and successful private equity-backed chief executives. Rather than viewing the following list as a kind of assessment 'skeleton key' to be used as an infallible point of calibration for chief executives in any deal, the reader is invited to consider the characteristics below in light of their own experience.

4.5.1   Decision-making and Problem-solving Ability

The decisions made by the chief executives are arguably some of the most critical in the life of the investment. Probably the most important characteristic which a successful chief executive can possess in this area is versatility. Where sufficient data are available to allow rigorous analysis, the individual needs to have the ability to work through these in a thorough and systematic manner. It is also important for them to feel comfortable making decisions in more ambiguous situations where data may be incomplete or contradictory. Successful chief executives also show versatility in the extent to which they collaborate with others. They often have an instinctive feel for situations in which it is appropriate to collaborate with others, and at such times are able to manage and facilitate effective discussions to arrive at an answer – as part of this, they are willing to be challenged by members of their team. They are also able to identify those situations where the best approach is for them to decide alone. There is some overlap here with the characteristics of a typical private equity investor: characteristics which they would share with a chief executive would include a high level of intellect and very strong analytical skills. However, in general, chief executives would differ in the extent to which they are able to bring creative and innovative thinking skills to bear and in some instances make them slightly more comfortable taking major decisions under conditions of uncertainty.

4.5.2   Emotional Control

Another defining characteristic of the most successful chief executives of private equity-backed companies is a high level of grounded confidence and self-assurance. They are able to convey a sense of being 'at ease' with themselves and aware of their limitations and, when appropriate, are not afraid to discuss these. This self-confidence can also mean that they are not afraid to challenge other stakeholders in the business, including the general partners, and the degree of lively discussion or even conflict generated is not something to be avoided. Many private equity investors will have encountered less confident chief executives who put on a brave face while feeling inwardly uncertain or who lack the conviction to challenge general partners. A further element on the level of emotions and values which they would share is an extremely strong work ethic and level of drive. The most effective chief executives are also able to manage their energy carefully.

4.5.3   Drive and Passion

A characteristic commonly shared by the successful chief executives is a very high level of ambition and an absolutely relentless determination to achieve their goals. They are also absolutely passionate about the business they are running and able to convey this passion to others.

4.5.4   Leading the Development Agenda

Given the immense pressure which leaders are subjected to on the route to exit, it can be tempting to dismiss the leadership development agenda as 'extra-curricular'. However, in order to ensure that leaders throughout the business are able to step up to the challenge and negotiate the necessary changes, it is essential that leaders at every level look at how they can develop themselves and empower and develop their people. Some of the most successful chief executives are the ones who engage with, and act as a figurehead and sponsor for, leadership development at all levels.

4.5.5   Ability to Form Interpersonal Relationships

In the area of interpersonal relationships, versatility again is the key characteristic. The most successful chief executives are able to form effective relationships with individuals from all levels of the organisation. They have the confidence and gravitas to deal effectively with the most senior individuals and act in a persuasive manner and project a sense of conviction.

They also have the ability to engage effectively with people at more junior levels and make themselves open and approachable. This versatility and flexibility in forming social relationships can be critically important during critical times as it helps the chief executive to be a reassuring presence to others. There is something of a contrast here with the archetypal general partner in a private equity fund. Whereas private equity investors are almost invariably effective at dealing with individuals who share their intellect and senior status, many struggle when trying to engage with people at more junior levels.

4.5.6   Self-awareness

The final characteristic shared with the most successful chief executives is a high level of self-awareness and the ability to understand how they are impacting those around them.

4.6   THE IMPORTANCE OF CONTEXT

In the previous sections we have set out three dimensions on which it is important to assess individual leaders as part of the leadership risk mapping process. Under each of these we have set out some of the generic skills and characteristics which generally contribute to the success within the context of private equity-backed businesses. It is, however, important not to generalise too much, as leadership risk is ultimately a function of how particular leaders perform within a particular business. The process of deciding what to assess at an individual level therefore requires that the specific business case and strategy are understood from a leadership perspective. As an illustration of how this process might work, we have set out below three common strategic scenarios and, for each one, provided illustrative examples of the kind of competencies, personality traits and motivational drivers which could enhance or impede leadership performance.

4.6.1   Strategic Scenario 1 – Cost Cutting and Improved Efficiency

In the case where the strategic plan centres on identifying operational efficiencies and radically cutting costs within the business, it would be important to assess senior leaders in the following areas.

Examples of relevant competencies
- Analytical ability – the ability to gather and process data efficiently and effectively in order to drive decisions.
- Decisiveness – the ability to make and implement decisions within a tight time scale.
- Communication – the ability to deliver difficult news and explain difficult decisions in a way which does not diminish the motivation of those who remain in the business.

Examples of relevant personality traits
- Tough minded – a preference for logical rather than compassionate decision making.
- High appetite for control (no great desire to collaborate).
- High emotional resilience.

Motivation
- Someone for whom affiliation and friendly relationships are not a primary driver as this could make it difficult to act on tough people decisions.

4.6.2   Strategic Scenario 2 – Product Innovation

In this scenario success depends on thinking laterally and resourcefully. The competitive advantage of the business depends on finding and selling novel solutions.

Examples of relevant competencies
- Creative thinking – the ability to spot new connections, find innovative solutions and think laterally.
- Collaboration – facilitating creative group discussions and encouraging lateral thinking in others.
- Adaptability – the ability to steer the organisational changes triggered by innovations and forge a creative culture in the business.

Examples of relevant personality traits
- Openness to new ideas.
- Enthusiasm – to pioneer new initiatives.
- Creativity and lateral thinking.
- Inner determination.

Motivation
- Someone driven by the need to create something new.

4.6.3   Strategic Scenario 3 – Customer Intimacy

In this scenario success depends on being able to establish a very close relationship with customers and be seen as being highly responsive to their needs.

Examples of relevant competencies
- Relationship building – the ability to establish and cultivate strong relationships. Being able to read others and manage interactions with them carefully.
- Delivery – being absolutely passionate about delivery and doing whatever it takes to ensure the customer's needs are met.
- Empowerment – being able to empower others further down the organisation so that they can deliver.

Examples of relevant personality traits
- Outgoing and gregarious.
- Empathetic.
- Active and energetic.

Motivation
- Someone with a passion for delivery.

4.7   SUMMARY

- Assessment at an individual level is at the core of the leadership risk mapping framework. In essence, the assessment of individuals needs to answer two basic questions: 'Can they do it?' and 'Will they do it?'
- Given the complex influences on human behaviour, the framework assesses individuals on three dimensions: competencies, traits and motivation.
- The dimension of leadership competencies looks at the skills and abilities which the individual has. Competency frameworks are useful in thinking through the links between behaviour and business performance. However, competences also have limitations as they do not explain the causal links between behaviours and outcomes and can encourage a generalised view of leadership effectiveness. It is also important to recognise that some competences have a 'shelf life' and overuse of a competency can lead to executive derailment.
- Psychological traits relate to the inner psychological preferences of the individual. Awareness of the individual's inner psychological landscape is important as it helps in understanding how they tend to perform key tasks such as making decisions, framing problems

and dealing with others. For leadership risk mapping purposes, it is important not to get lost in the complexity of human psychology. Using a simple model, such as the 'big five' personality characteristics, should suffice.

- The third dimension to assessment at an individual level is motivation, which relates to the inner drives and motives of the individual. Motivations can change over time and may not even be clear to the individual themselves. Although it is often assumed that financial gain is a prime motivator in private equity investments, this should not be seen as an end in itself. It is possible to discern a broad range of human motivations. From a leadership risk mapping perspective, it is important to ensure that the motivations of individual leaders are aligned with the leadership agenda of the business.
- The four quadrants of awareness can provide useful prompts in deciding what to assess in each of these key dimensions.
- There are some characteristics which are associated with effective private equity-backed chief executives across a range of situations.
- As well as identifying which general characteristics need to be assessed, it is important to look at the specific business strategy in behavioural and leadership terms and think about the competences, psychological traits and motivational aspects which would be most relevant.

REFERENCES

Smart, G. 1999. 'Management assessment methods in venture capital: an empirical analysis of human capital valuation', *Venture Capital* **1**(1), 59–82.
Van Velsor, E. and Brittain Leslie, J. 1995. 'Why executives derail: perspectives across time and cultures', *Academy of Management Executive*, Vol. **9**, No. 4.

5

Conducting Assessments at an Individual Level

Risks associated with conducting assessments at an individual level include:

- The approach is seen as threatening or intrusive and leads to bad feeling between the investor and the management team.
- The individuals being assessed become defensive and give a distorted view.
- The approach is not properly tailored to meet the overall purpose of the assessment.
- The approach fails to identify accurately 'false positives' and 'false negatives'.
- The assessor attempts to reach conclusions before all the data are gathered so important information is missed.
- Too much emphasis is placed on gathering data from one approach.

5.1 INTRODUCTION

As mentioned in the previous chapter, the aim, when assessing senior individuals as part of a leadership risk mapping exercise, is to gather information and raise awareness in order to answer two questions:

- 'Can they do it?' – do they have the capability and potential to perform at the level required.
- 'Will they do it?' – do they have the motivation to deliver and is there anything else which could interfere with or inhibit performance.

Once careful consideration has been given to the combination of competencies, traits and motivations upon which key individuals need to be assessed, the investor/assessor is then confronted with the challenge of how to approach the assessment. In finding the best approach it is useful to refer to the four quadrants of awareness discussed earlier. On the level of the 'outer' world, the assessment process needs to form a basis upon which the profile of each key individual can be framed within the context of the leadership challenges which lie ahead on the path to exit. The key here is to enable the investor and the members of the investee management team to identify factors which will facilitate successful leadership of the business and also identify any gaps, development needs or potential inhibitors to success. It is also critical when deciding on the best approach to assessment to give adequate consideration to the 'inner' world of both the investee management team and the investor. In terms of the inner world of the individuals being assessed, it is important to remain sensitive so that the techniques used do not feel overly intrusive or threatening and the process as a whole works in a way that strengthens rather than damages the relationship between the investor and the investee. In terms of the inner world of the investor, it is important that the assessment process provides a basis for testing any hypotheses which stem from the investor's instinct and gut feeling about members of the investee management team and provide a depth of reassurance that they really understand the key members of the senior management team as fully as possible. In line with other elements of the leadership risk mapping framework, it is suggested that the individual assessments draw on data from a range of sources. Ideally, the assessor should arrive at a position where it is possible to compare and triangulate the perspective of the individual him or herself ('self' perspective) with the views of others ('others" perspective) and relevant elements of the surrounding context. The approach to be adopted in exploring each of these perspectives depends to a large extent on whether the review is done as part of pre-deal due diligence or whether it is a review of an existing portfolio business. The suggested data strands used to build a picture of the relevant dimension of each individual can be summarised as follows:

	'Self' perspective	'Others" perspective	'Context' perspective
Competencies	Interview or discussion Curriculum vitae	Multi-rater assessment – 360-degree questionnaire or feedback interviews	Business case Job description Discussion Performance data
Psychological preferences	Psychometric questionnaire and/or psychological interview	N/A	N/A
Motivation	Interviews Motivational questionnaire	Feedback interviews	N/A

As can be seen from the above, the suggested approach to the assessment at an individual level centres on three components:

- A one-to-one discussion or interview with each individual.
- A feedback-gathering exercise.
- Some form of psychometric assessment.

Each of these components of the approach is described in detail in the following sections.

5.2 INDIVIDUAL INTERVIEWS

Some kind of extended one-to-one discussion with each individual will normally form the cornerstone of the individual assessment. Although many private equity investors will be extremely experienced in conducting individual interviews, it is important that this stage of the process is given very careful consideration. As mentioned above, a key consideration which will determine the tone and structure of the individual interview is whether it is taking place as part of a pre-deal management due diligence process or as part of a review of an existing portfolio business. The implications of these two scenarios are set out below.

5.2.1 Pre-deal Due Diligence

If the leadership risk assessment is being conducted before the deal has taken place then it will inevitably have an undertone of being some kind of 'test'. In reality, a detailed management assessment of this kind is not, and arguably should not be, the basis for whether a transaction takes place or not. If the investor has serious concerns about the capabilities of the management team this will generally lead to the deal being rejected at a much earlier stage. It is therefore more likely to be the case that the reason for conducting the review is to identify factors which will be useful for both the investor and the investee management team to be aware of once the deal has taken place in order to maximise the chances of success. Nonetheless, from the perspective of the investee team's 'inner world', undergoing a rigorous review of this kind is likely to feel like a 'high stakes' undertaking, on which a great deal depends and it will therefore be associated with a degree of anxiety. It is important to bear this dimension in mind when considering the best approach to take when interviewing.

There is evidence from the world of recruitment to suggest that the most effective kind of interviews for predicting future success are structured interviews. In contrast to unstructured interviews, which have the form of free-flowing discussions in which the interviewer asks questions as and when they occur to him or her, structured interviews follow a rigid format and consist of carefully worded questions. Here, the interviewer often has a pre-prepared score card which is used to mark the interviewee based on their responses to questions. Structured interviews are often used in order to assess people on the kind of leadership competencies which were described in the previous chapter. The technique typically involves working through one competency at a time and asking the interviewee to provide two or three examples of the situations in which they demonstrated skill in the area in question. Although the empirical evidence indicates strongly that this technique is effective and is certainly preferable to unstructured interview techniques, it has certain drawbacks and may be unsuitable within the context of leadership risk mapping. One fundamental problem with highly structured interviews is the way in which the structure itself tends to dominate. If the interviewer is hoping to gather data on three or four competencies, the line of questioning can become extremely repetitive and wearing for the interviewee. Moreover, there is a high level of transparency around which areas are under review and this could increase the risk of the interviewee manipulating their responses in order to create a good impression. Within the context of a leadership risk mapping process it is therefore likely that the stilted and artificial tone of a highly structured interview may compound the experience of being tested and impair the relationship between the investor and the investee rather than enhancing it. This then presents something of a challenge, as neither the unstructured nor the formally structured interview is particularly well suited to the situation under discussion. One solution is for the interviewer to use the rigorous preparation of the structured interview and maintain a clear view of the other areas where data needs to be gathered, but to internalise the actual structure so that the tone of the interview is much closer to a normal conversation. Whilst this means that the interviewer has to work much harder, it makes for a much more comfortable experience for the interviewee. This technique revolves around formulating a number of questions, often as much about the business as they are about the individual, and then allowing the discussion to flow from there in a way which will yield a range of insights about the individual. For example, the interviewer might ask

"What do you see as the biggest challenges facing the business?"

The interviewee's response could provide insights into one or more of the following areas:

- How far ahead they think.
- The balance of strategic and tactical insight.
- How optimistic/pessimistic or realistic they are.
- Whether they focus more on the inside of the business or the outer environment.
- To what extent their view is consistent with the view of other members of the team.

Other questions, for example 'where do you see yourself in five years' time?', can reveal how hopeful and confident they feel about the likely success of the present venture as well as giving valuable insights into what motivates them and what their ambitions are.

By working through a set of similar questions to this, the interviewer is able to reveal layer upon layer of insights about the individual. This can be illustrated in Figure 5.1.

In practice, conducting an interview in this way can be quite challenging and it takes practice before the interviewer is able to strike an appropriate balance between gathering the necessary detail and maintaining what feels like having a normal conversation about the business. One way to facilitate the process is to use two interviewers who alternate over the course of the conversation. This allows one person to manage

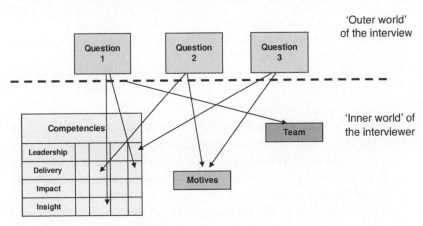

Figure 5.1 Interviewing in depth

the discussion whilst the other listens carefully and captures data on several levels.

5.2.2   Individual Discussion as Part of a Portfolio Review

If the leadership risk assessment is conducted on the management team of an existing portfolio company then, in contrast to the management due diligence scenario described above, it is questionable whether in fact an 'interview' is appropriate or necessary. The individual will have had the opportunity to demonstrate their effectiveness in leading the business and the investor will therefore already be much better acquainted with them. In this scenario, the one-to-one discussion may be more effective if it is managed more as a facilitative feedback session. As we will explore further in the next section, for portfolio businesses, it is probably better to gauge an individual's effectiveness and key competencies through the use of multi-rater feedback. In this instance, the individual discussion can be used as an opportunity to work through the feedback data and review outputs from any psychometric instruments which have been completed within the context of the challenges the individual is currently facing as well as their leadership agenda over the next 12 to 18 months. This makes for a collaborative and supportive tone and encourages personal ownership of the development agenda which emerges.

Considerations Under the Four Quadrants of Awareness

The four quadrants of awareness can be used to provide prompts to ensure that interviews and discussions are as effective as possible:

Investee's 'outer' perspective
- Ensure the interview questions are clearly linked to the business.

Investor's 'outer' perspective
- Ensure the discussion covers all the areas identified in the preparation phase.

Investee's 'inner' perspective
- Even if extensive briefing has been given, always set the scene at the start of the discussion, provide a reminder of the overall process and its purpose, and check whether there are any questions.
- Be aware of any topics or questions which appear to provoke an emotional reaction.
- Try to tune in to the individual's mood and manage the tone of the discussion accordingly.

Investor's 'inner' perspective
- Resist the temptation to start interpreting responses during the discussion – remember that the review and address phases come later, once all the data have been gathered.

5.3   MULTI-RATER FEEDBACK

In line with other elements of the leadership risk mapping framework, the perspective of 'others' can be an extremely useful point of reference when conducting assessments at the level of the individual. This is because it provides a point of comparison with the person's own view of themselves and it also makes it possible to build a picture of how the individual is seen in a live working environment. The extent to which it is possible to access feedback from others and the means of doing this depend again on whether the review is being completed as pre-deal due diligence or as part of the portfolio review. The different approaches for gathering data under the two different scenarios are described below.

5.3.1   Portfolio Review

If the assessment is being conducted as part of a review of an existing portfolio company, then it is entirely legitimate and appropriate to build into the process some kind of 360-degree feedback. The significant benefit of doing this is that it provides live feedback, rooted in the specific context of the portfolio business itself, and is therefore likely to provide the richest and most accurate view of the individual's performance on key competencies, as compared to extrapolating from past performance or relying solely on the individual's own evaluation of themselves. A range of approaches is possible here, depending on the time and budget available to do the review. The richest feedback of all is to be gained by conducting personal interviews with a range of respondents who have direct experience of working with the individual. Typically, the individual would nominate three or more of their peers and direct reports together with a line manager (if applicable) and possibly a range of external stakeholders. Each of the nominated respondents would then be interviewed for between half an hour and an hour, during which time detailed feedback on the individual would be gathered in a discussion covering all the relevant areas identified in the preparation phase. Feedback from the interviews is then summarised in a document, which can be discussed with the individual. Whilst this approach can be extremely useful in raising awareness and provide an excellent basis for development planning, it is also a highly sensitive process. If it is undertaken, the following areas must receive careful consideration. Firstly, it is important for all participants to understand that the feedback will be given in a non-attributable manner so that their particular feedback will not be traceable back to them. It is for this reason that there must be at least three respondents in any one respondent group. The exercise should also be managed, and the interviews conducted, by an impartial third party. If the investor is conducting the review in-house, the feedback interviews should be conducted by someone who does not otherwise have direct involvement with the business in question. As with other interviews, it is vitally important that there is careful preparation and a clear set of objectives behind each of the interviews. An alternative to feedback interviews is to administer an online 360-degree feedback questionnaire in which respondents (a similar respondent group to that described above) provide a numerical rating to indicate their feedback on the various relevant competencies which have been identified. The scores are aggregated and summarised by computer, which then generates a feedback report. Although this approach does not allow for the same depth and richness of interview-based feedback, it is less time-consuming and labour-intensive and therefore more efficient. If this approach is used it is important that the questionnaire allows respondents to provide narrative feedback comments as well as their numerical scores.

5.3.2   Pre-deal Assessment

If the review is conducted as part of pre-deal management due diligence it is not normally appropriate to use the kind of 360-degree feedback approach described above. Although it is not unusual to ask members of the management team to make feedback comments on one another, and this can provide useful data, given the wider context surrounding the review it may be difficult for individuals to be entirely candid in their feedback. Moreover, feedback at this stage will inevitably relate to an individual's performance within the context of the business before the investor became involved. The most common source of multi-rater feedback used during pre-deal due diligence is management referencing. Arguably, this is neglected in many forms of managerial selection, although it is becoming common practice in the area of management due diligence for private equity investors. Again, having a proper structure when interviewing referees is essential in order to tease out important details, such as how an individual responded to crises and in which areas his or her weaknesses required support from others. References can come from a number of sources: colleagues, other industry players, suppliers, customers and former employers.

A distinction needs to be made between named and unnamed references. If, during the interview, the interviewee mentions the name of a former boss, this person may be a good individual to contact for a reference. It is also useful, and perfectly legitimate, to used unnamed sources. Investors and assessors will have a personal network and perhaps someone in that network can shed light on the effectiveness of the particular individual in a previous post.

A further option, which has emerged over the last few years, is the possibility of conducting online reference checking. There are now a number of firms who specialise in doing background checks and providing what amounts to a 'CV audit'. Once the individual has given their consent, these organisations will check aspects of the CV such as education and professional qualifications. Such investigations are not expensive and can add an extra level of security to the referencing process. They should not, however, be viewed as an alternative to interview-based reference checking which can provide much richer information.

Considerations Under the Four Quadrants of Awareness

The four quadrants of awareness can be used to provide prompts to ensure that multi-rater feedback is gathered and used as effectively as possible:

Investee's 'outer' perspective
- Ensure the interview feedback questions are clearly linked to the business.

Investor's 'outer' perspective
- Ensure the feedback discussion covers all the areas identified in the preparation phase.

Investee's 'inner' perspective
- Ensure the respondent fully understands the overall process and address any questions before the discussion begins.
- Be sensitive to the relationship between the investor and the person giving feedback. Reassure the respondent about the anonymity of their feedback.

Investor's 'inner' perspective
- As before, resist the temptation to start interpreting responses during the discussion – remember that the review and address phase comes later, once all the data has been gathered.
- Do not allow any one feedback interview to taint subsequent ones.

5.4 ASSESSING PSYCHOLOGICAL TRAITS

As mentioned in the previous chapter, psychological traits and preferences may or may not be obvious on the surface. One of the most effective ways to understand the psychological preferences and traits of an individual is to make use of some kind of psychometric questionnaire. Such questionnaires can be administered in pen and paper format, although it is generally more efficient if they are completed online. The idea of using psychometric questionnaires can provoke a range of reactions on the part of private equity investors. In the recent past, when the increased volume of private equity-backed deals led to a growth in the market for management due diligence, research suggested that some investors were either sceptical or actively hostile to the use of psychometrics. Typical criticisms and reservations included:

- They do not predict performance.
- The results are too easy to fake.
- They make those taking them feel as though they are being tested.
- The dimensions they measure are not relevant.

In light of these and other reservations, many investors may resist using psychometric tools. However, as described in the previous chapter, from a leadership risk perspective, insights into psychological preferences can be extremely helpful in building a full picture of the individual. Much of the resistance to the use of psychometrics can be traced back to a failure on the part of those administering them, on the one hand, to explain the instruments adequately and, on the other hand, to understand properly the business context in which they were being used. The resistance can also be traced to wider tension and occasional mutual suspicion which sometimes exist between the world of finance and the world of psychology.

When psychometric instruments are used properly, they can yield extremely valuable insights, but care must be taken to give sensitive consideration to the following areas:

- They should be used selectively – it is better to select two or three relevant instruments, which can be completed in under an hour, than put individuals through a battery of tests which take half a day to complete.
- Ensure the instruments are not overly complex. When the results are fed back to the individual, the discussion should be mainly about the person rather than the instrument.
- Select instruments which are more descriptive than evaluative to reduce the feeling of being 'tested'. It is important not to confuse personality instruments, which highlight individual preferences and help to frame those preferences in relation to an 'average' person, with aptitude tests, where answers are either right or wrong and the aim is to assess intelligence. The latter are not generally appropriate for use in leadership mapping and, if they are used, extreme care should be taken.
- The questionnaires should be administered by qualified and experienced experts. This means they not only have the requisite psychological qualifications but also the necessary business insight to be able to put the results into context.

If it is felt appropriate to explore the psychological dimension in greater depth, then feedback on the psychometrics can be combined with a more in-depth psychological interview with a business psychologist. Such a discussion can be useful, not just in raising awareness around core psychological preferences but also in helping the individual to understand and integrate the other feedback data. The approaches which business psychologists are able to draw on when conducting a leadership risk mapping review are discussed further in the final chapter.

Considerations Under the Four Quadrants of Awareness

The four quadrants of awareness can be used to provide prompts to ensure that psychometric instruments are used as effectively as possible:

Investee's 'outer' perspective
- Ensure the use of the instruments is set in context – if it is not possible to give a clear explanation of the link between the

instrument and the overall goal of the exercise (and, indeed, the resulting business benefits), then it probably should not be used.

Investor's 'outer' perspective

- Be clear about the links between the instruments used and the relevant dimensions identified in the 'prepare' phase.
- Be careful in the choice of third-party experts to administer and feed back the instruments. Ensure they have sufficient credibility when putting the results into context.

Investee's 'inner' perspective

- Ensure thorough briefing and communication to minimise the feeling that they are being 'tested'.
- The individual should never feel 'forced' to complete the psychometric instruments if they are at all uncomfortable with them.
- Investor's 'inner' perspective.
- Try to temper any innate biases against the use of psychometrics.

5.5   REVIEW OF AVAILABLE DOCUMENTATION

A further source of data on one or more of the dimensions described in the previous chapter can be various documents which might be available. It is more likely that documentation will form part of the picture if the review is being conducted as part of pre-deal due diligence, where access to the individual may be limited and there is a shortage of direct information. Examples of the kinds of documentation and how they might be used include:

- *Curricula vitae* – can provide an overview of past experience and achievements. Asking questions about the CV and key career choices can provide useful insights into values and motivation.
- *Job descriptions* – can give a sense of key skills and competencies.
- *Performance data* – will summarise the kind of objectives the individual has been working towards and the extent to which these have been met. Again, this may provide insights into the level of competence and motivation.
- *Statements of operating performance* – if the individual played a major role in leading the business and driving results, the business results can give an indirect measure of effectiveness.

Although document review can provide insights useful in individual assessments, this is at quite an abstract level. Data in the documents should always be checked and verified and any conclusions which are drawn about the individual on the basis of document reviews should be carefully tested through comparison with the findings from more direct methods described above.

A review of key individuals in terms of their role and importance to the organisation may also be informed by considering the results of reviews which may have been conducted to assess other kinds of risk. For example, a broader review of operational risk may have identified individuals who are especially significant to the business or who are associated with a particularly high level of risk. Examples could include:

- Individuals who manage key relationships (for example, with key customers or suppliers).
- Individuals who have specialist knowledge.
- Individuals who have specialist skills.
- Individuals for whom there is no obvious replacement.

This kind of review of the broader operational risk landscape, although peripheral to the assessment of leadership risk, can be extremely valuable. It may be that such a review highlights key individuals who, although not obviously in the senior leadership population, should nevertheless receive special attention and may therefore also be considered within the scope of individual reviews.

5.6 SUMMARY

- In order to assess individuals in sufficient depth, it is important to gather data from multiple sources for each of the dimensions to be assessed.
- Individual discussions or interviews form a cornerstone of the assessment process.
- If the review is done as part of pre-deal due diligence, a discussion with the individual will inevitably feel more like an interview.
- It is important for the interview to feel neither too unstructured nor too structured. The best approach is for the interviewer to internalise the underlying structure so that the discussion feels like a conversation about the business.

- An individual discussion conducted as part of a review of an existing portfolio business can be much more of a collaborative process, involving a joint exploration of the data gathered.
- Again, the four quadrants of awareness can be useful in planning and managing this discussion.
- Another, extremely useful, form of data is provided by multi-rater feedback.
- For reviews of existing portfolio businesses, multi-rater feedback can be gathered through a 360-degree review, either based on interviews or using an online questionnaire.
- For pre-deal due diligence, multi-rater feedback would normally come from management referencing.
- Psychological preferences are best assessed through the use of psychometric questionnaires which can be administered online.
- Some private equity investors are highly resistant to the use of psychometric questionnaires and some of their criticisms are quite valid.
- However, if they are used properly, psychometric questionnaires can yield important data.
- A further source of data is provided by the existing documentation, such as CVs and job descriptions.
- Beyond members of the senior leadership team, it may also be useful to conduct individual assessments of other key individuals who, because of the wider operational risk profile of the business, are of special significance.

6

Deciding What to Assess at a
Team Level

Risks associated with establishing what to assess at a team level include:

- Undue emphasis on the personal aspects of the team, so that insufficient attention is given to other factors influencing their team effectiveness.
- False perception of what level of team performance can reasonably be expected, leading to an idealised view so that the team is assessed against unrealistic measures.
- Failure to establish which team to assess, so that the review focuses on the wrong people.
- Insufficient evaluation of the links between team beliefs and business performance, meaning that criteria upon which the team is assessed are not relevant.
- A static view of the characteristics of the team, so that the business 'outgrows' a particular team configuration without this being noted.

6.1 INTRODUCTION

It is important to recognise that there are a number of critical activities that take place above the level of an individual, no matter how experienced and talented, which can have a significant effect in terms of creating and destroying value in a business. Even if a business is very much the creation of a single entrepreneur, this individual will have a team supporting him or her. Many of the major decisions about the way the business is run are made on a team level and, when problems arise, these are often dealt with on a team level as well.

The basic questions which drive the decision about what to assess and explore in assessing leadership risk at a team level are the same questions relating to individual assessment. Ultimately, leadership risk at a team level is a function of whether the team have the potential to perform well enough to achieve the desired business results, and whether there are any factors which could cause interference and so prevent them from realising that potential. However, the challenge of assessing at a team level is potentially much more complex as there are many facets of a team which can influence performance and therefore many more dimensions and variables which need to be understood. In many ways the ability of the business to reach a successful exit is a function of the performance of its top team. If the team is operating effectively, it will formulate and deliver a strategy which will carry the business through exit and propel the business through unexpected challenges and obstacles. However, weaknesses at a team level may actively inhibit the performance of the business and drain the time and energy of its team members. The aim of this chapter is to set out the key determinants of team performance as a means of deciding what needs to be assessed in order to build a clear picture of leadership risk at a team level.

6.2   WHICH 'TEAM' TO ASSESS

It is important first of all to be clear about the way in which the word 'team' is used for the purposes of leadership risk mapping. For our purposes, the word 'team' is used to describe the group of people who are jointly responsible for leading the business and making its most significant decisions. In practice, this may be a board of directors, an operating board or a management committee. In terms of the size of the group, it will usually be three or more people and less than about eight or ten.

From a leadership risk perspective, it is the substantive responsibilities and activities of that group, rather than its legal form, which are of most importance in the context of management due diligence. Although a board may function as a team, with a high level of interdependency and collaboration, in some organisations the working group or team which acts as the 'engine' from which the business is driven may be elsewhere.

Having addressed the fundamental question of which team needs to be assessed, a second general factor to bear in mind is where that team is in its lifecycle. There are a number of possible scenarios, and some of the most common are listed below.

It may be the case that the top team which has already been running the business will continue to do so, in which case the assessment will be conducted on an intact team. Another possible scenario is that the team is more or less the same one which has been running the business, but with a key difference. A typical example of this is a management buyout, in which case it could be that the founder and/or managing director of the business is selling the business to his management team. In this scenario, a member of the existing team may be promoted and is thus making the transition from being a peer to the team leader. This will have potential implications for the dynamics of the team.

A further scenario may be that two groups come together. Perhaps a small board of directors is expanding by bringing in the heads of divisions in the business to form a larger management team. Another scenario may see representatives of the private equity fund coming into the business to join or manage one or more teams.

Clearly, the top team must be appropriate for where the organisation is at this stage of its evolutionary path. The team that came together around a founder entrepreneur to get a business up and running may not be the ideal team to steer the venture through a new phase of growth through acquisition. There may be historical or emotional reasons for certain individuals being part of a team, for example being close to the founder, or representing a particular stakeholder or shareholder group. These factors should all be explored during the assessment process.

The scope of this chapter precludes working through every possible team scenario which may arise. Instead, we will aim to highlight the key themes and issues which can arise at a group level and which are most relevant from a leadership risk perspective. Whichever team scenario the investor is looking at, team-level assessment should provide answers to questions such as:

- Is this the right team to manage the business, realise its strategy and take it through to exit?
- Does each team member have a clear role and area of responsibility?
- What does each team member bring to the team?
- Is each member clear about what the team's views are on common goals and values?
- How do the team members complement one another?
- Which stakeholder groups do the team members represent?
- Are there any gaps in the team? If so, where do these exist and what are the implications?
- What are the key risks relating to the team?

Once there is clarity as to which team needs to be assessed and where the team is in its lifecycle, it is possible to draw again on the four quadrants of awareness model introduced earlier. On the investee side of the model we will outline below the key dimensions about which decisions need to be made when planning what to assess. From the 'outer' perspective we will look at the team's sense of purpose as well as the structure and process which is in place to achieve that purpose. From the 'inner' perspective we will discuss the opaque but often critical dimension of team dynamics. We will then go on to highlight relevant considerations from the investor's side. Firstly, from the 'outer' perspective, we will look at how the investor can go about exploring the links between the various dimensions of the team and the ultimate performance of the business. From the 'inner' perspective we will look at the dynamics which may exist between the investor and the investee management team.

6.3   THE OUTER VIEW OF THE INVESTEE TEAM

6.3.1   Purpose

One pivotal aspect of the investee leadership team which will need to be assessed is the extent to which it has a clear purpose. In the broadest sense, the purpose of the top team relates to the overarching mission of the business – why the business exists and what it is hoping to achieve. From a leadership risk perspective it is vital to gauge the extent to which members of the top team share a clear and compelling vision of what the business is about and where it is heading. Clearly, a lack of clarity at this level can profoundly inhibit the capacity of the team to move the business forward and it cannot necessarily be assumed that the same vision is shared by all team members. Beyond the overall purpose of the business it is also important to build a clear picture of how that vision will be achieved. On the one hand, this relates to the strategy which will be adopted – the markets which will be focused on, the key axes of competition and differentiation, and the way in which value will be generated. It also relates to the core values which will underpin how the business is operated. It is essential that the top team have a clear shared picture on each of these areas, which will then inform the way in which they lead their respective parts of the business. Differences of opinion are not necessarily dangerous, and it is often healthy to have a team where alternative perspectives are represented. However, it is important that such differences are made explicit, so that they can be explored and resolved within the team.

Leadership risks relating to team purpose include:

- Energy, attention and organisational resources are directed to the wrong areas.
- The leadership team stalls over key business decisions.
- There is no clear strategy.
- The values followed by team members and others in the organisation are not consistent with business goals.
- Priorities and key decisions are not aligned with high-level business goals.
- There is no compelling vision for the rest of the business, or there are mixed messages.

The following are examples of questions on team purpose which might be asked as part of a leadership risk mapping exercise:

- Does the team have a clear sense of purpose, a vision of what they want to achieve?
- To what extent is that vision shared by all members of the team?
- Is there a clear sense of what differentiates the business from the competition?

6.3.2 Structure and Process

Another critical 'outer' facet of the team is the set of processes which the team uses to manage the business and manage itself. In order to assess the adequacy of the team's processes to manage the business, it is important to establish the sufficiency and relevance of the inputs into the team and the effectiveness of its outputs. In terms of the inputs it is critical that the team has access to relevant and sufficient management information about what is happening within the business and how well the business is performing, as well as stringent information relating to the environment in which the business operates which will enable the team to identify and respond appropriately to risks and opportunities. Inputs should also be sufficient to provide accurate feedback for the management team on the basis of which they can reflect and fine-tune their management of the business in order to ensure that it remains on track. Such feedback needs to provide an appropriate balance between 'hard' financial data and other, more qualitative information about factors such as what is happening within the business on a cultural level and how the business is performing against the expectations of different external stakeholder groups. It is also important to understand how clearly the team's internal processes are defined, as this will influence how well it defines and uses the inputs and how effective they are in managing outputs and achieving the outcomes which they aspire to. Key processes include factors such as how the team organises itself, how often it meets and how those meetings are managed and how decisions are made. It is also important that the team has adequate processes in place to ensure that differences of opinion can be properly aired and resolved.

Leadership risks relating to structure and purpose include:

- The structure does not match the size and direction of the business – either too much structure which hampers the team or too little meaning so it is not properly organised and not in control.
- Inputs are not sufficiently detailed or relevant to provide a clear view and a sound basis for decisions.
- The team draws on too many inputs and gets bogged down in complexity.
- There are insufficient feedback channels so the team cannot accurately gauge their effectiveness.

The following are examples of questions on team structure and process which might be asked as part of a leadership risk mapping exercise:

- How is the team organised?
- What is the optimal structure and process, given where the business is now and the way it will develop on the route to exit?
- Are team processes clear to all team members?
- What are the key inputs which the team uses to manage the business?
- Do the inputs used provide a sound basis for decisions?
- How effective is the team at making decisions?
- How does the team monitor its effectiveness – what sources of feedback are used?

6.3.3   Team Governance

Related to the systems and processes which serve to maintain the team's vital functions is the way in which the senior team manages the

Figure 6.1   Governance overview
Source: Garratt, 2003.

governance agenda. Businesses can go a long way while functioning in an ad hoc fashion without formal processes in place. But as the level of complexity increases, and the organisation becomes bigger, systems, processes and the governance of the business overall must evolve to keep up. One important element of business-level assessment involves looking at what systems, processes and governance the organisation has in place to ensure that it runs effectively.

Bob Garratt provides a clear overview of corporate governance in his book *The Fish Rots from the Head*, where he contends that a company's success or failure is determined by the performance of its board. His overview of policy formulation in an organisation serves as a useful framework against which to assess an investee business in terms of governance, both as it is now and when considering what it will need to look like as it delivers a new strategy. See Figure 6.1.

Garratt's model breaks the policy formulation of an organisation into four quadrants, looking at two primary functions – compliance and performance – internally and externally, and within the short term and long term. Compliance (short term) consists of the broad areas of accountability and supervising management internally. Performance (long term) entails policy formulation and strategic thinking. In considering each of Garratt's dimensions, the investor should ask what the investee firm has traditionally done in each area, what they do currently and where they tend to focus. It is important to ensure that the function of each area is achieved adequately given the current situation of the business.

Policy Formulation and Foresight

This quadrant encompasses clarifying the organisation's purpose, vision and values, and emotional climate and culture – what Garratt calls the 'heart of the firm', which serves as the touchstone for the way the firm operates. While it sounds very obvious, not all firms are clear on what their purpose, or fundamental reason for being, is. Vision and values also reside in this quadrant. Garratt defines values as beliefs in action. Values can be translated into a set of behaviours which each employee can be assessed and rewarded against, thus creating a powerful consistency throughout the organisation.

Developing corporate climate and culture takes place at many levels, both obvious and subtle. In tangible terms, these can manifest as a written code of conduct, stating which behaviours are acceptable within the organisation. The climate can be measured with employee satisfaction surveys, which give an indication of where there are issues within the company. Depending on its size and sophistication, it may have a government or public affairs function whose job it is to watch legislation and lobby to have the company's view heard with the relevant decision-makers.

Strategic Thinking

As discussed earlier in exploring this area, investors will want to gain an understanding of how the organisation cultivates its strategic thinking and what its annual strategy process looks like. More established firms will have a strategic cycle with key milestones throughout the year. This may involve carrying out SWOT analyses on a regular basis.

It should keep a close watch on those variables which impact its business, i.e. interest rates, demographic trends, etc. so that it can ensure it is optimally positioned within a changing environment. It is also critical that the board and management know exactly how and where value is added in the business. It must set corporate direction and constantly review and allocate vital resources.

Supervising Management

Overseeing management performance is essential for any business. This means having a clear set of targets and deliverables for management, against which their performance is measured and rewarded on a consistent basis. It is worthwhile looking into the firm's internal audit function and gaining an understanding of how it works and who it reports to.

Here, the investor will want to look at the associated people risks – to determine whether the firm has the organisational capability, the people and skills it needs to perform.

Accountability

This quadrant looks at how the company handles its responsibilities to its various stakeholders, from its shareholders and employees, customers, suppliers, legislators and the community. Processes, systems and governance should be in place to enable the firm to meet its obligations to each group. For example, one should look at the company's relationship with its customers and suppliers and how these are both managed via processes and systems, i.e. CRM systems, partnership agreements, tendering processes, etc.

Leadership risks relating to the team governance include:

- The team does not understand what governance is.
- The team only focuses on certain elements.
- There is a lack of clarity around some elements of governance.
- The inputs available to the team are insufficient to manage the governance agenda.
- The business has outgrown the governance procedures in place and more sophisticated governance is needed.
- The future strategy and/or business growth will require a different style or depth of governance.
- The team lack the time, knowhow or other resources needed to fulfil their governance responsibilities.

The following are examples of questions which may be explored in relation to team governance:

- How much time does the team spend on each of the four (Garratt) governance dimensions?

- For each dimension – do the team have the necessary data, time, knowledge and other resources to do what they need to?
- Is there a shared view of what the team need to do around governance?
- Does the team manage governance through a coherent and consistent cycle?
- How far does the team's governance process match the current and future size and complexity of the business?

6.3.4   Composition

A further, fairly explicit, facet of the team is the range of skills, experience and perspectives which the members of the team bring. Ideally, the members of the team will be able to complement one another in terms of skills and perspective. Between them they should have the necessary range of insight and knowhow to work through whatever issues arise in the business agenda on the route to exit. It is vital to ensure that the necessary checks and balances exist across the personalities making up the team. It is also crucial that there is a proper balance of perspective between individuals who focus within the organisation and those who look more to the external landscape. In this context it is important to recognise that qualities such as experience and expertise exist on more than one level. On the one hand, it is important that members of the senior team bring sufficient specialist or technical knowledge (for example, in areas such as finance, operations and marketing). It is also useful if they bring more general business experience and have the requisite skills and experience of leading and participating in senior teams. Such 'second-order' skills are important in cultivating a rounded and effective team. Having previous senior team experience will help to ensure that team members are effective at judging how best to contribute and challenge across all areas which impact the business. It is also useful if a range of perspectives are represented in the team with a range of outlooks from the prudent and pessimistic to the more creative or daring. Where different members of the team have different thinking styles and different ways of unpacking issues, this will help to ensure that problems and decisions are thoroughly explored. It is also important that different viewpoints are appropriately represented within the team, and that different stakeholder voices are represented and respected.

Leadership risks relating to team composition include:

- The team has an insufficient spectrum of skills and experience to tackle the full agenda facing the business.
- Team members only contribute to team discussions relating to their own area, meaning that opportunities for 'cross-fertilisation' of ideas are lost.
- Team members have insufficient experience of how to operate in senior teams.
- The team has a limited repertoire of problem-solving styles – all issues and problems are explored in the same way.

The following are examples of questions on team composition which might be asked as part of a leadership risk-mapping exercise:

- What range of skills and experience do team members bring and how well does this match the business agenda?
- How far do members of the team complement one another in terms of perspective and outlook?
- How wide is the repertoire of thinking styles in the team?
- How willing are team members to contribute to discussions outside of their main area?

6.4 THE INNER PERSPECTIVE – TEAM DYNAMICS

Another dimension which is particularly important on the personal level is team dynamics, which stem from the interplay of the individual personalities that comprise the team. From a risk point of view, dynamics can play a pivotal role and can have a significant impact on the effective functioning of the team and the decisions the team makes, especially when they are under pressure. However, this dimension of the team dynamics is often one of the hardest to gauge as it exists at a deep level and is far from static. Moreover, it is hard to find a definitive view of what is meant by 'dynamics'. One aspect relates to the general 'climate' within the team and whether members feel generally positive about the team and their fellow team members. Related to this is the general level of energy in the team and whether or not members feel they derive energy from participating. A further component of team dynamics is how different members of the team act and react in relation to one another and how the different personalities play off one another and whether certain individuals tend to dominate. Rather than having a single cause, team dynamics have a variety of causes including:

- The history of the team and its membership and what patterns have developed over time.
- The political currents running through the team and the different interests of team members.
- The clarity and suitability of the overt dimensions of the team (such as purpose, structure, processes, etc. – see above).
- The psychological characteristics of members.

Leadership risks relating to team dynamics include:

- The team acts as a drain on members' time and energy.
- Interpersonal differences get in the way of effective team functioning.
- Some members of the team exert a disproportionate influence.
- There are some topics and issues which the team is unable to address.
- Team members have insufficient understanding of each other.
- Because of a lack of mutual trust and/or respect, team members do not feel able to rely on each other.
- There are cliques and factions within the team which drive their own interests before the wider business interest.
- Some team members feel marginalised and do not contribute fully as a result.

One factor which mitigates the risk that team dynamics impede performance is the extent to which the team is willing periodically to look reflectively at itself and invest time and attention in its own development. If this is not something which has been done before, then a team assessment conducted as part of a leadership mapping exercise can provide an excellent springboard from which to launch a team development agenda.

The following are examples of questions on dynamics in the team which might be asked as part of a leadership risk-mapping exercise:

- What is the 'climate' within the team?
- Does participation in the team energise team members or drain them?

- Is there mutual respect and support among members?
- Are there any 'taboo' issues which the team finds it difficult to discuss?
- How quickly can the team move on after disagreements?
- Is there a healthy balance of participation and influence in the team or do some team members tend to dominate and others keep quiet?

A critical dimension of team dynamics is the level of trust which exists amongst team members. Where trust exists this can provide a bedrock for cooperation and effective performance and enable the individual members of the team to really get the best from one another. However, trust is a fragile thing and very difficult to 'measure' objectively. In deciding what to assess, a starting point is to look at how far the opinions and behaviours of the individual members of the team reflect an underlying level of trust.

The following are examples of questions on trust in the team which might be asked as part of a leadership risk-mapping exercise:

- Do members of the team communicate with each other in an honest and open manner?
- Do members of the team feel 'safe' within the team – for example, are they comfortable admitting mistakes and discussing their weaknesses?
- Is there mutual respect among team members?
- Are differences of opinion and conflicts managed in a helpful fashion?
- Do members of the team hold themselves and one another to account?
- Do people feel that the team and the business operate fairly?
- Is there a general willingness to work for the greater good?
- Do team members feel confident that they can rely on their colleagues during times of difficulty?
- How easy is it to integrate new members into the team?

6.4.1 The Team Leader

When looking at team dynamics, it is useful to explore the particular role of the team leader. When deciding what to assess at a team level, it is important to consider the individual who is charged with leading the team and how they and the team interact. As in other areas of leadership risk mapping, context is crucial and it can be dangerous to assume that there is a 'template' for an ideal team leader. Instead, it is useful to consider the following risks and questions in connection with the leader.

Leadership risks relating to the team leader include:

- The team lack confidence in the leader.
- The role and expectations of the leader are unclear.
- Uncertainty exists as to who the leader is.
- The leader is overly domineering and suppresses team discussion and collaboration.
- The leader lacks the necessary authority to fulfil the role.
- The leader lacks the necessary characteristics to lead the team.

The following are examples of questions which may be explored in relation to the team leader:

- How long has this person been the team leader and what was the history to their appointment?
- What style of management do they use and how does this fit with the team?
- Do the leader and the rest of the team have the same priorities and agenda?
- Is it clear who the team leader is?
- Are there any unofficial leaders and, if so, who are they?

6.5   THE OUTER VIEW OF THE INVESTOR

As with other areas of the leadership risk-mapping process, in planning what to assess at a team level it is important for the investor to consider fully the implications for team performance which arise from the strategic plan of the business. There may be a temptation to plan the review with a preconceived assumption about which team to assess (for example, assuming it has to be the board) and which will be the relevant aspects of the team to look at. However, it is important to tailor the focus of a team review to the specific leadership journey which the team will have to navigate. Different strategies and different scenarios will imply different challenges for the management team. If, for example, the strategy implies significant innovation then the collective creative capacity will be significant. If it is expected that the business will make a number of major acquisitions, then it will be particularly important for the team to be both resilient and well organised to ensure that the acquisitions are managed quickly and effectively whilst causing minimum disruption to the ongoing business. It is also important as part of this 'outer' investor perspective that the investor derives maximum benefit and insight from their own previous experience. Here again, the diligent exploration of what they have learned from previous investee management teams can be of great benefit. It may be useful to reflect on the most and least successful management teams which they have worked with previously, and to explore what the team characteristics were which distinguished these two groups. Investors may also usefully draw upon their own personal experience as members of teams. By the time the review is conducted, the investor will also have had direct experience of the investee team and this may provide clues on which areas could usefully be probed during the review. If the team review is carried out as part of pre-deal due diligence, the investor can reflect on what they noted about the team. For example, the way they interacted with each other during roadshow presentations. It could be, for example, that certain members of the team appear to dominate whilst the role of other team members appears to be unclear. Similarly, if the review is to be conducted on an existing portfolio company there will be an even greater bank of direct experience upon which they can draw. Here, the investor will have a clearer sense of the key inputs and outputs of the team and be able to formulate questions as to the links between team and business performance.

6.6   THE INNER VIEW OF THE INVESTOR

When planning a team-level assessment it is important that the investor is sensitive to the dynamic which exits between them and the investee management team. A common and important consideration arises here, where representatives from the investor come to sit on the board of the investee business. In deciding what to assess it can be very useful for the investor to look reflectively at themself and their preferred style of dealing with investee management teams in order to gauge the impact that this may have. In deciding which aspects of key dynamics to explore, the investor may want to consider how receptive the team is likely to be to new participants. It is also useful if the investor is sensitive to unspoken doubts or criticisms they may have about their investee management team in order to ensure that these can be either confirmed or refuted through the assessment process without interfering with it and without impairing the relationship with the team.

6.7 SUMMARY

- The challenge of deciding what to assess at a team level is more complex than in individual-level assessment as there are many more dimensions and variables to consider.
- The performance of the top team as a whole can significantly improve the chances of business success but when the team is not working it can drain the time and energy of participants.
- The first step in planning team-level assessment is to be clear about which team needs to be assessed. The focus should be on whichever group forms the engine through which the business is driven, major business decisions are made and key challenges addressed.
- It is also important to understand the history and current status of the team and how long it has existed in its current form.
- Again, the four quadrants of awareness can provide a useful framework around which to plan team-level assessment.
- The outer view of the investee should focus on the following:
  - The overall purpose of the team.
  - The structure and processes it uses to manage itself.
  - Its governance procedures.
  - Its composition in terms of the range of skills and experience which its members bring.
- There are particular considerations which need to be borne in mind in relation to the leader of the team.
- As well as outer dimensions it is also important to look at the deeper level of the dynamics of the team, what the climate is within the team and the impact of this.
- Looking from the outer perspective of the investor involves reflection on what needs to be understood and assessed in the team given the strategic plan they will have to work through.
- The investor should also allow their direct experience of working with the team to inform the agenda for assessment.
- In terms of the investor's inner perspective, it is important to remain sensitive to the dynamic which exists between any representatives of the investor who sit on the management team and the team that they are participating in.

REFERENCE

Garratt, B. 2003. *The Fish Rots from the Head*, Profile Books.

7

Conducting Assessments at a Team Level

Risks associated with conducting assessments at a team level include:

- The approach is so intensive that it undermines trust in the team.
- The approach serves to compound rather than relieve tension in the team.
- There is insufficient transparency about what techniques are being used and the purpose of the review, which provokes suspicion and defensiveness in the team.
- A failure to triangulate the data on the team from different sources leads to a distorted view.
- The approach fails to gather data on all relevant dimensions of the team.
- The approach is not aligned with the priorities identified in the planning phase.
- The approach is perceived as putting the team in an artificial situation, which is unrealistic and seen as a waste of time.

7.1 INTRODUCTION

Given the significant complexity associated with team performance and the various facets, both visible and invisible, performing a robust and accurate assessment at team level can represent a significant challenge. As with other areas of the leadership risk-mapping framework, the approach set out in this chapter is based upon the idea that, to build a rich and useful picture of something as complex as a team, it is important to draw on and triangulate multiple perspectives. The challenge of assessing the team is further compounded by the fact that access to the team as a whole will probably be even more limited than access to individual team members. It is therefore necessary to strike an appropriate balance between gathering sufficient information, whilst not wasting time or testing the patience of the team members. As with other areas of the leadership risk-mapping framework, the solution here is to have a well-thought-through plan and systematic process.

Key considerations to bear in mind when assessing at a team level include the following:

Time available – how much time do the team have available to participate? How to make best possible use of that time?

Access – how much access to the team is it reasonable to expect?

Clarity – questions should be as clear as possible.

Transparency – whilst questions should be absolutely clear, it is important not to provide too much detail about the underlying rationale and the putative leadership risks prompting the assessment as this may interfere with the process.

Tone – the assessment should be conducted in a way which feels collaborative and supportive.

Future oriented – although data can only be gathered on the past and present of the team, from a leadership risk perspective, the future implications should always be considered.

To maintain a clear overview of the team assessment it is often useful to set up an assessment matrix. One side of the matrix shows the various facets of the team which are to be assessed (as described in Chapter 6). The other side of the matrix is made up of the different assessment techniques which will be used to provide multiple perspectives on the team. Each technique may be used to gather data on one or more facets of the team, so that successive layers of data can be compared and triangulated in the review phase. Some of the most useful methods of gathering data on teams and team performance are the following:

- Individual interviews conducted with the team members.
- Feedback questionnaires on the team completed by team members and other stakeholders.
- Existing documentation on the team and its members.
- Aggregated data on individual team members:
  - from the psychometric instruments;
  - from competency assessments;
  - from 360-degree feedback.
- Team-level psychometrics.
- Observation of the team (both 'in vivo' and 'in vitro').

The following matrix summarises how these various data sources (shown on the horizontal axis) can be applied to build a picture of the various team facets described in Chapter 6 (shown on the vertical axis).

	'Self' perspective	'Others'' perspective	'Context' perspective
Purpose	Interviews Questionnaires	Interviews Questionnaires	Document review (e.g. vision and mission statement, strategic plans, press reports, etc.)
Structure and Process	Interviews Questionnaires	Interviews Questionnaires Observation	Document review (e.g. organisation chart, minutes)
Composition	Interviews Aggregated psychometrics	Interviews Observation Aggregated competency assessment and 360-degree feedback	Document review (e.g. history of the team, changes in membership)
Governance and Policy	Interviews Questionnaires	Interviews Questionnaires	Document review (e.g. different outputs from the planning cycle)
Dynamics	Interviews Questionnaires Observation – with facilitated debrief	Interviews Questionnaires Observation	N/A

The remainder of this chapter provides a detailed description of each of these assessment techniques, with details of how they can be applied to the various facets of the team and the possible advantages and disadvantages of each.

7.2 INTERVIEWS WITH TEAM MEMBERS

Members of the leadership team will usually be interviewed as a matter of course as part of their own individual assessment. The early stages of these individual interviews (i.e. the first few questions) can be an ideal time in which to ask team members for their views on the team and its strengths and weaknesses. In the (unlikely) event that no individual assessments are to be done, then one-to-one interviews with team members are still important as it is the collected themes from these individual interviews which form the core of the 'self'-evaluation of the team. In compiling a guide for conducting these individual interviews it is therefore useful to include questions on the various facets of the team. Examples of typical interview questions are given below.

Sample questions on team purpose:

- 'Describe the team's high-level vision for the business.'
- 'Define the team's top priorities.'
- 'What are the core challenges facing the team?'

Sample questions on structure and process:

- 'How is the team organised – what are the key processes?'
- 'How does the team decide what to focus on?'
- 'How are key decisions made – can you talk me through a decision which the team has made?'

Sample questions on team composition:

- 'What do different people bring to the team?'
- 'How does the team ensure that problems are explored from all perspectives?'
- 'Do you feel there are any skills missing or underrepresented in the team?'

Sample questions on dynamics:

- 'How would you describe the mood in the team?'
- 'How are disagreements handled in the team?'
- 'How has the team changed over time?'
- 'What needs to change going forwards?'

Once all answers to these questions have been gathered from all members of the team, it is interesting to compare them to establish whether team members share a common view of how the team works and the challenges which it faces. Individual answers are, almost by definition, a reflection of what each individual finds important. Comparing these individual responses provides a valuable overview of the team, highlighting areas of clear agreement as well as areas where opinions are more varied.

7.3   INTERVIEWS WITH OTHER STAKEHOLDERS

Depending on the scope and purpose of the leadership risk assessment and the perceived importance of the team dimension, it may be useful and appropriate to conduct interviews with other stakeholders who are not members of the team but have direct dealings with it (common examples being non-executive directors or people whose line managers are members of the team). As in other areas, it is important to be sensitive to the trade-off which exists between the value of the views of other stakeholders and the time and effort needed to elicit these views, as well as the degree of access which the reviewer has to other stakeholders. If it is decided that interviewing other stakeholders is important, for example if there are significant concerns about the team's effectiveness or if interviews with individual team members have yielded conflicting or surprising information, then it might be useful, for example in the case of a board, to interview some or all of the non-executive directors. As well as the specific questions detailed above, it can also be useful to ask other stakeholders more general questions around what they see as being the key strengths and weaknesses of the team and what, if anything, concerns them about the team.

7.4 FEEDBACK QUESTIONNAIRES

The use of questionnaires to gather feedback on the perceived effectiveness of the team from various dimensions can provide very useful insights. Moreover, the questionnaires can be designed so that they are not too time-consuming to complete and relatively easy to administer. Probably the most crucial consideration when preparing to use a team feedback questionnaire is to ensure the questions are framed in a way which will yield the most useful and relevant information possible. Although it may appear unnecessarily time-consuming to design a questionnaire for each leadership risk assessment and, in practice, it will probably be the case that the questionnaire used in most reviews will centre on a very similar set of common questions, in order to maximise the opportunity of raising awareness in the right areas and minimise the associated leadership risks, it is always important to critically review the questionnaire in light of the specific goals of the review in question. Listed below are the key factors to have in mind when preparing and administering a team feedback questionnaire.

7.4.1 Format of the Questions

One common and useful way of formulating questions is to phrase them in terms of statements and then invite respondents to rate the statements on a scale of 1 to 5. For instance, an example of an item to be circulated to members of the team could be 'we prepare effectively for team meetings' and respondents could then express their feedback using the scoring key ranging from 1 – Not at all, to 3 – Sometimes and 5 – Always. It is also useful to formulate the questionnaire so that members of the team can rate themselves individually (under a 'Me' column) and the team as a whole (under a 'Whole Team' column). As in many other areas, there is a tendency to rate oneself higher than the group and by providing an opportunity to separate out these two perspectives it is possible to get a clearer view. The above format can usefully be applied to capture 'self'-evaluations from members of the team across a number of dimensions.

If feedback is to be invited from other stakeholder groups, a slightly different format can be used. For example, it may be the aim of the questionnaire to determine where the team currently focuses attention and where it is felt the team ought to focus attention. Here the questionnaire would begin with a general instruction to respondents along the following lines:

> Please evaluate the degree to which the team currently focuses on each of the following areas and also how much focus the team should place on these areas ideally.

The questionnaire will then provide two columns for respondents, a 'current level of focus' column and an 'ideal level of focus' column and again a 1–5 rating scale ranging from 1 – Not at all to 5 – A great deal. At the end of the structured questions it is also useful to provide a space in which respondents can make any further comments in narrative form.

7.4.2   Content

It is possible to design a questionnaire which covers most of the facets of the team referred to in the previous chapter. However, it is important to be selective and it is generally useful to restrict the number of questions to around 30 or 40 so that the questionnaire can be completed fairly quickly and with a high degree of focus on the part of the respondent. In practice, a questionnaire to be completed by the members of the team should contain around four to six questions on each of the following areas:

- Purpose
- Structure and process
- Composition
- Team climate (dynamics).

Rather than listing the questions under these headings, once they have been formulated it can be good practice to mix them up so that the respondents are more inclined to give impartial and objective views rather than being influenced by what they might see as the underlying purpose and perspective of the question. A further set of questions of the second type described above (relating to focus) could be completed by members of the team as well as other stakeholders. Here, four to six items for each element of the business agenda should suffice (for example, long-term vision, business performance, identifying and managing risks, growing the business, managing and developing the team).

7.4.3 Questionnaire Administration

Questionnaires can be administered in a number of formats, including pen and paper, soft copy (as email attachments) and online. Whichever medium is used, it is important that the questionnaire is administered in such a way as to preserve the anonymity of respondents whilst still making it possible to determine which respondent group they belong to (whether they are members of the team or other stakeholders). For this reason it is important that there is an absolute minimum of three people in any respondent group, and preferably five or more.

7.5 EXISTING DOCUMENTATION

A wide variety of existing documentation from other parts of the business can provide information on the senior team and its effectiveness. Whether or not it is possible or realistic to use certain documents will depend on the context surrounding the leadership risk review. Clearly, if the review is done as pre-deal due diligence it is likely that there will be restricted access. Even if the review is done on an existing portfolio business, some documents may not be easily available. For the purpose of the current discussion, however, it is useful to indicate some of the key documents which may be available and the kind of information on the team which they may yield:

- *Strategic plan* – should provide information on the overall purpose of the team, quality of decision making or clarity of strategic thinking.
- *Organisation charts* – can provide information on team composition and the responsibilities and accountabilities of team members.

- *Vision and mission statements* – as the 'official' view of where the company is heading, can provide an interesting point of comparison with the perspective of individual team members.
- *Board minutes* – as an indicator of where the team focuses energy and attention and the level of participation of different team members.
- *Staff surveys* – as an indicator of how the team is perceived within the wider organisation.
- *CVs and written profiles of board or team members* – as an indication of past experience and team composition.

7.6   AGGREGATE DATA FROM INDIVIDUAL TEAM MEMBERS

By consolidating data on individual members of the team it is possible to build a 'bottom-up' picture. Care should be taken not to extrapolate such summaries too far, and this perspective should always be compared with data gathered from other sources (as described elsewhere in this chapter). However, such analysis can be useful in identifying dimensions of similarity and difference amongst team members and may provide clues to the roots of conflict or dysfunction within the team. In the following sections we describe three different types of individual data which may be aggregated to provide a team overview.

7.6.1   Aggregating Psychometric Data

As we discussed in Chapter 5, a sensitive and judicious use of psycho-metric questionnaires can play an important role in raising awareness of the 'inner world' of leaders within the business. If psychometric data is available for individual members of the management team it is possible to aggregate these in various ways, which can provide extremely useful insights into what is happening within the team. At a simple level the individual reports from the various psychometric instruments can be compared in order to highlight similarities and differences. If all members of the team share similar profiles, this may contribute to a feeling of harmony and consensus within the group, although it may also highlight collective blind spots. If most of the group share a similar profile whilst one or two members are at the other end of the scale on certain key personality dimensions, this may help to explain common patterns of disagreement within the team.

It is also possible to unpick the individual scores on various psycho-metric instruments and combine these to produce 'maps' of the team relating to key areas of team functioning. Such maps are most effective when they are produced selectively in order to highlight the key dimensions of the team which are most relevant given the business agenda and leadership challenges which they face.

7.6.2   Aggregating Data on Individual Strengths and Weaknesses

If detailed assessments have been conducted on an individual level and these contain 'benchmark' evaluations of team members against key competencies, then it may be helpful to calculate the overall average score for the team on each competency. As described above, this will provide an overview of the team in terms of overall areas of strength and possible weak spots. However, such summaries should be treated with caution as they represent a summary of something which is already at a summary level. Moreover, such summaries give, at best, an overview of the team's potential so must be considered alongside possible sources of interference in order to establish what level of performance they may imply.

7.6.3   Aggregating 360-degree Feedback

If an automated online 360-degree feedback questionnaire has been used then it can be a relatively easy matter to use the computer which hosts the 360-degree review to produce a consolidated report for the team as a whole with average scores for each item and summary reports.

One advantage associated with using aggregated individual data on the team is that the data are already available and do not have to be specially gathered. Another advantage is that each of the three types of individual data described above is relatively objective, so provides a counterpoint to the subjective opinions of team members. However, combining data in this way can mean that it becomes oversimplified and loses some of its 'texture'. The mathematical processes involved in calculating averages inevitably pull scores towards the middle. As a result it is preferable, if possible, to prepare team summaries where the individual scores are still discernible (here, it will be necessary to remove team members' names).

7.7   LIVE OBSERVATION OF THE TEAM

All of the techniques described so far involve gathering data about the team in fragments which are then assembled in order to build a picture of the team as a whole. The technique of actually observing the team in action provides an immediate, 'live' view which can be very enlightening. There are two basic scenarios for team observation, either or both of which can be used within the context of a team-level leadership risk assessment. The first option is simply to observe the team 'in vivo' going about its ordinary business, for example holding a board meeting or perhaps making a team presentation. The second scenario is to observe the team 'in vitro', whereby the team is requested to participate in one or more group activities, the specific purpose of which is that they can be observed and assessed. Both scenarios are discussed in further detail below, along with the pros and cons of each. One critical factor to bear in mind, whichever scenario is employed, is that the observer/assessor is appropriately prepared well in advance of their observation of the team. It is important to draw on considerations from the 'Prepare' phase in order to establish a checklist of those facets of the team on which data is to be gathered and what they would like to find out about each of those facets. It is best to have a written description of the various themes and topics against which notes can be made during the observation. Examples of the kind of questions which may be explored on different facets of the team are as follows:

On process
- How quickly and effectively is the team able to get on with its allotted task? To what extent do team members become distracted?
- Is there a clear structure and purpose to the meeting?

On team composition and participation
- Does every member of the team participate appropriately?
- Are different views and opinions aired?
- Does the team discussion allow for fair examination of issues from different perspectives?

On team dynamics
- What is the emotional climate within the team?
- Is there appropriate use of humour?
- Does there appear to be mutual respect?
- Do some individuals appear to dominate and close down discussion?
- Do there appear to be factions or cliques within the team?

A list of questions should be established based on the overall purpose of the exercise and the priorities which have been identified. Depending on the context, the observer may or may not reveal which aspects of the team they are going to observe. Having looked at how best to prepare for a team observation exercise, we can now explore the two scenarios in greater detail.

7.7.1 Observation of the Team in a 'Live' Environment

At whatever point in time the team-level assessment is conducted, it is likely that the investor will have at least some opportunity to observe the management team in action. If the review is to be conducted as part of pre-deal management due diligence, one opportunity may arise if the team is making a roadshow presentation or question and answer session. If the review is conducted on an existing portfolio company, it could be that the investor already participates in board meetings as a board member or could request to sit in on a board meeting. The key advantage of using live observation of the team is that it provides the most realistic view possible. It also has the advantage of not requiring any extra time from the team (as they would be having the meeting anyway and the meeting will not appear contrived). However, there are potential disadvantages or areas of possible concern associated with this scenario. Firstly, even though the team meeting observed is 'real', the very fact that team members know they are being observed and assessed will almost inevitably have an impact. Certainly in the opening stages of the meeting it is likely that members will attempt to present themselves in a positive light and 'be on their best behaviour'. If the observer remains as unobtrusive as possible and the meeting is allowed to run for a sufficient length of time and with a sufficiently engaging agenda, such observer effects should subside. Another potential disadvantage is that the agenda and format for the team interaction had, by definition, been established for a different purpose than simply for the team to be observed. The team agenda may not therefore provide the observer with sufficient opportunity to gather the information they require on the facets of the team which are being observed.

7.7.2 Observation of the Team in a 'Test' Environment

The alternative to observing a live team meeting is to gather the team and request that they complete one or more exercises, the specific aim of which is to raise awareness of how they function as a team. It is not uncommon to employ such a technique when a team is being assessed as part of pre-deal management due diligence. Depending on who is doing the assessment, a variety of approaches are possible here. At one end of the spectrum the team may be presented with a fairly abstract challenge or exercise (similar to group activities and games used as part of team-building events). This may involve building a model or solving a puzzle. Another possibility is to give the team a business case to work through where they have to make certain decisions on the basis of artificial business data. Finally, the team may be given a topic to discuss or a decision to make which is taken directly from their own business agenda. In practice, it is almost always better to use this latter type of activity as it tends to strike the best note with the team and hopefully will provide outputs which are genuinely useful to the business. The advantage of using such test exercises is that it is possible to manipulate the scenario in order to maximise the chances that the team will show certain facets of itself. This scenario also makes it easier for the observer to intercede or even facilitate exploration by the team of how it is operating. The disadvantage of this technique is that it may give a distorted view of the team, as the artificial nature of the situation may tempt them to put on a kind of performance. There is also a risk that requesting the team to participate in such an exercise may give rise to ill feeling, especially if the activity appears irrelevant – in which case the whole exercise may be perceived as a waste of time.

7.8   SUMMARY

- Conducting an assessment at team level is particularly difficult because access to the team is likely to be even more limited than access to individuals. Decisions about how best to assess on a team level should consider how much time and access is available and care should be taken to ensure the team is properly briefed.
- To build a rich picture of the team it is useful to gather and integrate data from a range of sources, including:
  - Individual interviews with team members.
  - Feedback questionnaires.
  - Review of existing documentation.
  - Aggregate data from individual team member assessments.
  - Team-level psychometrics.
  - Observation of the team.

- Interviews with individual team members require careful preparation. The various dimensions of the team described in Chapter 6 can be used to develop a comprehensive interview questionnaire.
- Questionnaires can also be used to conduct interviews with other stakeholders who see the team in action. Questionnaires on team effectiveness can be very useful. These allow team members to rate both themselves and the team as a whole on key dimensions of team effectiveness. Such questionnaires can also be used to build a sense of where the team focuses most of its energy and attention.
- Existing documentation – such as strategic plans, organisation charts, vision and mission statements, board minutes and staff surveys – can also provide valuable insights into the team.
- A further perspective can be gained by aggregating data already gathered on the individual team members, e.g. in terms of their psychological strengths and weaknesses.
- If possible, it is also very useful if the assessor can observe the team directly. One option is simply to observe the team conducting an ordinary meeting. Alternatively, the team can be requested to participate in a special exercise. In either case, it is important to do everything possible to ensure that 'observer effects' are minimised.

8

What to Assess at an Organisational Level

Risks associated with planning assessments at an organisational level include:

- The organisation lacks the potential to meet the needs implied by the strategy.
- The strategy founders due to lack of organisational knowledge or experience.
- The degree of organisational change implied by the strategy is underestimated.
- There is a failure to give adequate consideration to the cultural dimension of the organisation so underlying problems fester and then erupt.
- The route to exit is blocked by cultural issues such as resistance to change.
- There is a lack of commitment in the wider organisation to the new strategy and this goes unnoticed.
- Attempts by the investor to 'impose' a particular strategy are unsuccessful.

8.1 INTRODUCTION

The third and final level of analysis in the leadership risk-mapping framework is about building awareness of leadership risks which exist at a wider, organisational level. This level of analysis is arguably the most complex and least accessible of all. The wider organisation can be seen as the mechanism through which the strategy will be realised. It is the operation of the organisation which takes strategy from a set of abstract ideas and translates them into outcomes and, ultimately, business results. No matter how skilled the individual senior leaders of the business are and how effectively they operate as a team, unless they are able to engage with the wider organisation and harness its potential, they will struggle to lead the business to a satisfactory exit. The fact that the leadership team depend upon, and have to act through, the wider organisation represents a primary source of risk. Although the momentum of the strategy is positive and directed towards value creation, the organisational momentum may have a very different orientation. As Stan Lees points out in his book *Global Acquisitions: Strategic integration and the human factor*, all forms of organisation, including businesses, are subject to the law of entropy, which moves them towards a simpler, less complex form. The inherent risk posed by entropy is highlighted by the definition he cites from Katz and Khan:

> The entropic process is a universal law of nature in which all forms of organisation move towards disorganisation or death.

Ensuring that the force of entropy does not destroy the business requires energy and the more complex the organisation, the more energy is needed. The risk of entropy is minimised where the organisation is held in a steady state yet, as we have described in earlier chapters, private equity-backed businesses are almost always subject to change and the increased complexity which comes with rapid growth. Regardless of the specific business agenda in prospect, leaders will therefore always be confronted with the underlying risk of decay and disintegration of the very organisation which they depend on to achieve success.

Leadership risks at this level stem in part from the collective impact of the risks which exist at an individual and team level but there is also a broader dimension of risk which cannot be located within a particular person or team. Many of the factors which influence value creation and destruction at an organisational level are buried deep within the fabric of the business and its culture and do not easily lend themselves to assessment and analysis. In contrast to problems which exist at an individual or team level, it may be some time before problems which exist at an organisation level actually manifest. For this reason, the discipline of thinking through the potential risks well in advance in a thorough and systematic fashion takes on an even greater importance.

As with other elements of the framework, the variables from the 'inner game' equation provide a useful starting point in determining what to assess at an organisational level. Within the context of organisational leadership risk assessment, the key question relating to 'potential' is whether the organisation as a collective whole has the requisite skills and capacity to implement the planned strategy and achieve the best possible results on the route to exit. The possible sources of 'interference' stem to a large extent from the organisation's capacity to negotiate the various changes which will be required in order for it to successfully implement the strategy. It is, therefore, particularly important to identify, understand and address potential sources of resistance to change, many of which may be rooted in the culture of the organisation.

In the following sections, we have clustered the various factors which need to be considered when deciding what to assess at an organisational level under the 'four quadrants of awareness' referred to in earlier chapters. We begin by looking at the outer perspective of the investee and describe two aspects. Firstly, we highlight the importance of the strategic dimension and explain the significance of understanding the history of strategic thought and implementation in the organisation, the way in which the current strategy has been formulated and, looking forward, what kind of organisational capability will be required to implement that strategy in the future. The other component of the investee's outer world relates to the visible aspects of organisational culture such as physical artefacts, norms of behaviour and the basic 'logic' which underpins the way the business is run. In terms of the inner perspective of the investee, we explore some of the deeper, more cryptic facets of organisational culture. These include factors such as the meaning and significance which the organisation has for the people who operate within it and, on a deeper level, some of the unconscious beliefs and assumptions which underpin the business. In terms of the investor's outer perspective, we describe the value of looking critically at the strategic aspirations which the investor places upon the business and emphasise the importance of looking realistically at what the strategy will mean in practice for the organisation and what it will take to realise the growth and potential which is foreseen. We also set out some of the generic leadership risks which arise during periods of organisational growth and change, regardless of which strategy is being used to drive that growth. We highlight again the value which the investor can derive from reflecting on past experience with other investments to identify potential leadership risks at an organisational level. Finally, in relation to the investor's inner perspective, we recognise the valuable role which 'gut feel' can play as an indicator of leadership risks at an organisational level and also stress the importance of investors guarding against biased thinking which may distract them from considering the organisational dimension in sufficient depth.

8.2   INSIGHTS FROM THE FOUR QUADRANTS OF AWARENESS

8.2.1   The Investee's Outer Perspective

Strategic View

The natural starting point when considering the outer view of the investee business is the strategy. The strategy of the investee business forms the backbone of the business case for making the investment in the first place and provides the shared roadmap upon which the route to exit is charted. We have described in earlier chapters how, from a leadership risk perspective, the strategy should also be explored in terms of the behavioural and leadership journey which it implies and this type of analysis can also yield valuable insights at an organisational level. One way to 'unpack' the strategic agenda of the business is to look at it in terms of different points in time and to consider the past, present and future of strategy in the business.

In terms of the strategic past of the organisation, the aim is to build an understanding of the history of strategic thinking within the organisation, to form a picture of how strategic planning has traditionally been managed. For larger, well-established organisations, there may be a dedicated strategy function, whereas in smaller, newer organisations, there may be fewer formal strategic planning processes. The aim, in looking at the strategic past, is to gain an understanding of how far the organisation has thought strategically and how effective it is in acting on the results of that strategic thought and implementing its strategic plans.

Leadership risks stemming from the organisation's strategic past include:

- The organisation has no history of thinking strategically and has tended to be more tactical and reactive.
- Strategic thought in the organisation has been dominated by key individuals who have now left.
- Strategy has lacked sufficient depth and sophistication to enable the business to identify and pursue opportunities.
- The organisation has formulated strategy but has been unable to implement this successfully.
- Strategy formulation has been seen as a one-off event rather than an ongoing process.

The following are examples of questions relating to the organisation's strategic past:

- How sophisticated is the understanding of strategy within the organisation?
- How strategic has the organisation been?
- Where has the strategy tended to come from within the organisation?
- How has the organisation tested and developed its strategies?
- Is there a clear trail within the organisation from strategic formulation through to implementation?
- What has tended to get in the way of implementing the strategy?

As well as exploring the strategic tradition within the organisation, it is important to focus in particular on the genesis of the current strategic plan and assess the 'strategic present'. If the leadership risk-mapping exercise is being done as part of pre-deal due diligence, it should be ascertained whether a third party or group of parties, for example bankers, advisors or consultants, have developed the strategic plan in order to create a compelling case for the sale. If this is the case, it is important to assess how realistic and well-thought-through the plan is and to what extent the senior team were involved in its formulation. In another possible scenario, the vendor of the business may have developed a strategy prior to leaving the business but the people who are going to implement it are the team doing the buyout. In this case, it is important to ask how far the team understand the strategy if they did not create it themselves, and how far they agree with it. From a leadership risk perspective, it is inherently risky if the leadership team charged with implementing a strategy did not themselves formulate it.

Leadership risks stemming from the current strategy include:

- The strategy has been developed just to make a good impression or influence the sale of the business so it is unrealistic.
- The strategy has been set by outsiders and is not sufficiently rooted in the reality of the business.
- If the strategy has been formulated by third parties, the management team required to implement it either do not fully understand the strategy or do not agree with it.
- The strategy is so radical that it is untested within the organisation.
- The strategy has not been thought through in terms of more indirect consequences and unintended outcomes.

The following are examples of questions relating to the current strategy:

- What was the genesis of the current strategy?
- How new is the current strategy and how coherent is it in relation to the existing business?
- How far is the current strategy understood by the management team who will implement it?
- How far do the management team agree with the strategy?
- What might be the wider organisational consequences of the strategy?

Looking ahead at what will be required to implement the strategy going forward will provide yet more insights on the landscape of leadership risk. The delivery of the new strategy may require new skills and abilities and challenge people to think more strategically or more creatively. Leaders may need to think further ahead than they have done traditionally. They may have to expand their viewpoint to take greater account of external markets and threats. Decision-making processes may need to change, with decisions being taken faster, based on new criteria, in different parts of the organisation. Looking beyond the business results, it is important to step back and consider what potential impact (some of which may be indirect) the new strategy will have on the management team. Complexity may increase, which can have a knock-on effect throughout the organisation. Key stakeholders, such as customers, suppliers and other decision-makers, may also feel the impact.

Leadership risks stemming from the future implementation of the strategy include:

- The strategy requires growth at a level or rate which the organisation cannot match.
- The strategy requires skills and knowledge which are not available within the organisation.
- Hidden sources of resistance exist which could inhibit the implementation of the strategy.
- The transition from the existing strategy to the new one will cause major disruption to the business.
- Insufficient motivation and commitment to the strategy exists at different levels of the organisation which may jeopardise successful implementation.

The following are examples of questions which might be asked about the future implementation of the strategy:

- What skills and knowledge will be needed to implement the strategy?
- Do the necessary skills and knowledge exist within the organisation and how will any gaps be filled?
- What are possible sources of resistance to the changes implied by the strategy?
- How ready is the organisation to change and grow?
- How will the change process be managed so as to minimise resistance?

Culture

The links between organisational culture and business performance are far from straightforward. Indeed, the very term 'culture' is not universally understood and there are a variety of definitions. The extent to which organisational culture will influence business results varies depending on the particular business context but, from a leadership risk perspective, it cannot be ignored as it can represent a significant source of resistance to the implementation of strategy and the change which that may bring. It is therefore important to have an understanding of organisational culture which is sufficiently robust as to prompt useful questions and provide information on the potential risks without being too complex or abstract.

A useful model of organisational culture is provided by Stan Lees (see earlier reference) who built on the work of Smirich (1983) and Schein (1985) to suggest that culture can be seen as existing on five levels, where each level is less tangible and more opaque than the last. The first three of Lees' levels of culture can be framed within the 'outer world' of the investee as they are 'public'. The first, most tangible level relates to what Lees describes as 'artefacts and creations', which relates to the physical structures of the organisation such as its buildings and the layout of its offices. The main reception area, for example, is often highly reflective of the wider culture. The second level of culture relates to the way the organisation is structured and the norms of behaviour. Here, the culture can be reflected through the dominant styles of leadership, how people dress and how centralised the management is. The third level of culture which exists in the outer world relates to the shared logic which underpins the business – how people justify and explain the way the business is run and what are stated as being the core values of the business.

Each of these dimensions can provide a reflection of the organisational culture and can thus provide useful insights into where leadership risks may lie.

Leadership risks arising from the visible aspects of organisational culture include:

- The changes which need to be made are inconsistent with the observable, public facets of culture.
- Cultural artefacts are rooted in the past and are not consistent with where the business needs to be.
- In perpetuating the imbedded aspects of culture, people resist change so that organisational progress on the route to exit is impeded.
- Structures and behaviours in the business are inconsistent with the future strategy and will get in the way of organisational change.
- The new strategy requires new values and beliefs.

The following are examples of questions relating to visible cultural artefacts:

- What do the visible artefacts say about the business and will these have to change (buildings, office layout, etc.)?
- What is the predominant style of leadership and what are the other main styles of behaviour? How will these impact the business on the route to exit?
- How is the organisation structured and how will this have to change? What may be the consequences?
- What is the basic logic behind how people explain the way the business works?
- Does the new strategy imply a new set of explanations of how the business works?
- What are the values which guide decisions and actions within the business? Are these consistent with the new strategy?

8.2.2 The Investee's Inner Perspective

Significant elements of the leadership risk landscape may exist on a deeper, invisible level, and these can be a further source of resistance to change. Underlying doubts, fears or objections to planned changes may fester on a cultural level for some time before they become evident. It is useful here to consider the final two levels of culture set out by Stan

Lees in the framework introduced above. Lees' fourth level of culture relates to the meaning and significance which people in the business attach to symbols such as logos, what cars people drive and the benefits and privileges which they may enjoy. At this level, the culture may be reflected in key individuals who may be seen as organisational 'heroes'. A possible sensitivity may arise here if, for example, the founder of a business leaves as part of a management buyout as this person may be seen as a hero to others lower in the organisation who may then feel that their loyalty has been betrayed. This may be compounded if the private equity investor is perceived as a threat. In recent years there have been a number of critical stories in the press about private equity investors, so it could be that there is scepticism or even apprehension about the investor on a wider organisational level. This, combined with residual loyalty to the departing founder of the business, may prompt a crisis of cultural identity. Lees' final, deepest level of culture relates to unconscious assumptions which are taken for granted. By definition, these beliefs are outside the conscious thought of people in the organisation but may trigger powerful reactions if they are challenged. In the next chapter, we will draw further on the work of Stan Lees to set out questions relating to 12 unconscious organisational assumptions, which can be used to identify risks at this level.

Leadership risks relating to the invisible aspects of culture include:

- Changes seen as destroying a shared past which leads to resistance.
- The involvement of the investor is seen as a threat and triggers conflict.
- Changes are implemented in a way which is seen as breaching the basic assumptions underpinning the business so that people become demotivated or leave.
- Insufficient time and attention are allowed for the change to take place on a deeper, cultural level.
- Because change appears to be working on the surface, signs of resistance at a deeper level are overlooked and fester – only to erupt later.

The following are examples of questions relating to invisible cultural artefacts:

- What are the most resonant cultural symbols within the organisation and what meaning is attached to these? How can these be used to implement change successfully?

- What are the deeper hopes and fears of the organisation and how will these be affected by the change?
- What are the basic assumptions upon which the business has been built and how will the strategy on the route to exit impact on these?
- Who are the 'heroes' and 'villains' in the business who will be in the cultural spotlight going forward?

8.2.3   The Investor's Outer Perspective

One advantage which the investor brings is the insight which comes from having worked across a number of different businesses, with different strategies and in different contexts. For this reason, the investor may be better able to spot signs that the business may be experiencing 'growing pains', whereby the rate at which the business is expanding outpaces its existing systems and processes. Eric Flamholtz described a number of symptoms which may indicate that the business has become too big for its operational infrastructure and the investor should be alert to these as they may impact delivery of the strategy going forward.

Signs that a business is experiencing 'growing pains' include the following (from Flamholtz):

- People feel that there are not enough hours in the day.
- People are spending too much time 'putting out fires'.
- Many people are not aware of what others are doing.
- People lack understanding of where the firm is heading.
- There are too few good managers.
- Everybody feels 'I have to do it myself if I want to get it done correctly'.
- People feel our meetings are a waste of time.
- When plans are made, there is little follow-up and things just do not get done.
- Some people feel insecure about their place in the business.
- The business continues to grow in sales but not in profits.

It is also important from the investor's perspective to be sensitive to the risk that they are imposing an overly complex or ambitious strategy on the investee business. Considerable care is needed where the future strategy derives more from the thinking of the investor than the investee. As described above, whenever a management team is called upon to implement a strategy which is not their own this increases the risk that they may not fully understand it or be committed to it.

Finally, as with other areas of the leadership risk-mapping framework, it can be useful for the investor to reflect on past experience as a means of determining which organisational insights have proved to be most useful with other investee businesses and what the best way is then to bring these to the surface.

8.2.4   Investor's Inner Perspective

The investor should be careful not to dismiss cultural themes on the grounds that they are too intangible and unquantifiable. It can also be useful to reflect on feelings and messages which may trigger a gut feeling that there are underlying problems in the business and formulate these as hypotheses that can be tested through the leadership risk-mapping process. Finally, the investor should resist the possible bias of attributing problems to key individuals when the actual cause may exist on a wider organisational level.

8.3   SUMMARY

- The organisational level of analysis is arguably the most complex and least accessible dimension of the leadership risk-mapping framework.
- Regardless of how skilled the senior leaders of the business are, they are dependent on the operation of the organisation to achieve business results.
- Although the strategic momentum of the business is positive, all organisations are subject to the 'Law of Entropy', and energy and attention are required to ensure they do not descend into chaos.
- Some leadership risks at an organisational level stem from issues relating to key individuals or teams, but other leadership risks exist only at an organisational level.
- Leadership risk at an organisational level can be viewed as a function of the strategic 'potential' of the organisation to deliver the strategy and the existence of 'interference' often stemming from resistance to change which exists at a cultural level. In assessing what potential exists at an organisational level it is useful to examine the strategic past, present and future of the organisation.
- The strategic past of the organisation relates to how effectively it has been able to formulate and implement strategy previously.

- In exploring the strategic present of the business it is important to consider where the current strategy has come from and the extent to which the management team who will implement it understand and agree with it.
- In looking at the strategic future of the business from a leadership risk perspective, it is necessary to gauge what knowledge and skills will be required in the future to deliver the strategy and how far these exist within the organisation.
- The cultural dimension of the business also has significant implications for leadership risk. Organisational culture can be conceived as existing on different levels, some of which are visible and some of which are hidden.
- By exploring the different artefacts of culture it is possible to look for points of possible conflict with the planned route to exit and so anticipate sources of resistance to change.
- Regardless of the specific strategy which is being considered, from a leadership risk perspective it is also important to remain sensitive to signs that the organisation is suffering 'growing pains', indicating that the business is outgrowing its operational infrastructure. Investors should take care not to impose overly ambitious strategies on investee businesses and can benefit from translating organisational insights from past experience into the context of current investments.
- Investors should also take care not to be too quick to discount the organisational and cultural dimensions of their investments and too quick to blame problems on individuals.

REFERENCES

Flamholtz, E. 1995. 'Managing organizational transitions: implications for corporate and human resource management', *European Management Journal* **13**(1), 43.

Katz, D. and Khan, R.L. 1966. *The Social Psychology of Organizations*, John Wiley & Sons, Ltd.

Lees, S. 2003. *Global Acquisitions: Strategic integration and the human factor*, Palgrave Macmillan.

Schein, E.H. 1985. *Organizational Culture and Leadership*, Jossey-Bass.

Smircich, L. 1983. 'Concepts of culture and organisational analysis', *Administrative Science Quarterly* **28**, 339–358.

9

Conducting Assessments at an Organisational Level

Risks associated with planning assessments at an organisational level include:

- Assessment at an organisational level is conducted in a way which causes unnecessary disruption or triggers resistance to change.
- The assessment misses key dimensions of the organisation, such as the culture.
- The assessment fails to identify potential sources of resistance to change.
- The assessment provides an overly positive view so that the investor overestimates the organisation's capacity to change.
- The assessment does not provide a realistic view of how quickly the organisation will be able to manage change.
- The assessment does not raise awareness sufficiently to enable the investor to formulate a robust plan for implementing change.

9.1 INTRODUCTION

As described in Chapter 8, assessment at an organisational level represents a considerable challenge as there are so many variables which may impact on leadership risk, some of which are completely intangible. As with other elements of the framework, in addressing this challenge it is useful to think in terms of gathering and comparing information from multiple data sources. In the case of organisation-level assessment, the data sources can usefully be conceived as falling into two broad categories:

- 'Top-down' organisational data, which are gathered specifically in order to conduct the leadership risk assessment at an organisational level. Top-down assessment is discussed in the first part of the chapter.

- 'Bottom-up' data, which are gathered as part of the individual and team-level assessments but also provides insights into leadership risk at an organisational level. Bottom-up assessment is described in the second part of the chapter.

Whereas at least some 'bottom-up' data will be available in most leadership risk-mapping reviews, regardless of the context, the extent to which 'top-down' data gathering will be possible depends very much on when and why the review is being conducted. If, for example, the review is being conducted as part of pre-deal management due diligence, access to organisational data may be limited and it may not be possible to conduct the kind of organisational surveys which might be possible for existing portfolio businesses.

As described in Chapter 8, the two elements of the 'inner game' equation serve as a useful prompt in conducting organisational assessment, whereby factors relating to 'potential' stem from the organisation's capacity to deliver the strategy and negotiate the necessary changes necessitated and factors relating to 'interference' relate to resistance to change, particularly on a cultural level.

	'Self' perspective	'Others'' perspective	'Context' perspective
'Potential'	Extracts from individual-level assessments (*'Bottom up'*) Extracts from team-level assessment (*'Bottom up'*) Individual assessment interviews (*'Bottom up'*)	Interviews with other stakeholders (*'Top down'*) Employee satisfaction surveys (*'Top down'*)	Behavioural strategic review (*'Top down'*) Previous strategy documents (*'Top down'*) Documentation from previous change initiatives (*'Top down'*)
'Interference'	Individual assessment interviews (*'Bottom up'*) Dynamics between team and wider organisation (based on discussion and observation) (*'Top down'*) Culture surveys (*'Top down'*)	Employee satisfaction surveys (*'Top down'*) Focus groups (*'Top down'*)	Behavioural strategic review (*'Top down'*) Other organisational indicators (absentee data, customer feedback) – look out for underlying trends and signs of 'growing pains' (*'Top down'*)

Assessment at this level therefore entails gathering and triangulating data from a range of sources and perspectives. Although this is a delicate exercise, it needs to reflect the complexity of the organisation and an overly simplistic approach would merely provide a false sense of certainty. The following table provides an overview of the various sources of organisational data that will be described in this chapter.

We begin by looking at the organisation from the 'top-down' perspective.

9.2   THE 'TOP-DOWN' PERSPECTIVE

9.2.1   Strategy, Culture and Leadership Risk

Conducting organisational leadership risk assessment from the top-down perspective involves discussing, reviewing and reflecting on information relating to the organisation as a whole in order to determine what factors will help to carry the business through to the desired exit point and what might get in the way. The aim here is to maintain a view of the organisation as the mechanism through which the strategy will be translated from an idea into reality and so carry the business through to exit. Central to this process is the behavioural strategic review, which involves dissecting and challenging the current strategy from a leadership perspective to identify the leadership skills that will be required to deliver it and the leadership challenges it implies. We describe below how to approach such a review. We also show how interviews, reviews of existing organisational documentation and culture surveys can be used to enrich the top-down perspective.

9.2.2   Behavioural Strategic Review

The dimension of the organisation which the investor will be most familiar with is the strategic plan. If the leadership risk review is being conducted as part of pre-deal due diligence, then the strategy will be set out in the information memorandum and further details may be available in documents such as the commercial and financial due diligence reports. For reviews of portfolio businesses it is likely that even more detailed information on the strategy is available. To illustrate how the strategic plan might be used to conduct a behavioural strategic review, we set out below some broad strategic scenarios together with the associated leadership challenges.

9.2.3   Organic Growth

One way of categorising the many possible strategies for organic growth is to use the concept of 'value discipline', as set out by Michael Treacy and Fred Wiersema in their book *The Discipline of Market Leaders*. They distinguished between strategies of:

- Operational excellence
- Product leadership
- Customer intimacy.

We will use this classification to illustrate the kind of questions which an investor might raise in assessing the capacity to deliver the plan, as each of these routes to growth will imply different leadership challenges and risks.

Operational Excellence

Operational excellence is based on a strategy of providing the lowest-cost goods and services, while minimising any problems for the customer. One leadership challenge associated with this strategy is that of ensuring that transactions are managed efficiently, for example by ensuring that processes between the organisation and its suppliers are as streamlined as possible. The extent to which the organisation has effective measurements in place will be decisive, as will the processes for training and management of staff in how to operate efficiently. Companies that focus on operational excellence will usually provide a narrow range of products and services, so the extent to which this is actually the case, and how customer expectations are managed, should also be assessed. From a leadership perspective, negotiation skills will play a critical role in this scenario.

Typical questions arising from this strategy would include:

- How clear an insight do leaders have into what drives efficiency and reduces cost?
- How well calibrated is the dashboard leaders use to manage the business?
- Do leadership styles and practices ensure the most efficient approach?
- How well do leaders model and coach others in effective negotiation?
- Are leaders able to exert an appropriate level of challenge when dealing with customers?

Product Leadership

Organisations following a strategy of product leadership gain their business advantage by producing new and innovative products and services. As innovation will be central to this strategy, it is important to ascertain the extent to which innovation is encouraged, how open the management is to taking risks, and how successful the business is at attracting, growing and retaining innovative product designers. Here, leadership qualities such as creative thinking will be essential.

Typical questions arising from this strategy would include:

- How do leaders foster creativity within the businesses?
- How effectively are new ideas shared and explored?
- How well can the leadership team promote a nimble organisation? What could slow things down?
- How far ahead do leaders think and how widely do they look in identifying new opportunities?
- Do leaders give their teams sufficient latitude, freedom and space to think to allow them to generate new ideas?

Customer Intimacy

A strategy based on customer intimacy involves targeting one or more high-value customer niches, and focusing all possible efforts on building and maintaining a detailed understanding of customers' needs and meeting these. This approach calls for yet another set of processes, skills and behaviours, such as anticipating customer needs, potentially sharing risks with customers to develop new products and services, and developing the systems which will enable the business to be extremely responsive. In this case, relationship-building skills will be essential to success.

Typical questions arising from this strategy would include:

- How effective are leaders in tracking and managing customer needs?
- How closely is the organisation able to mould itself to match and react to the requirements of key customers?
- How sensitive are leaders to practices and structures which customers may find jarring?
- How do leaders promote a culture of responsiveness to the customer?
- How does the leadership team define the limits of sacrifices which the organisation is willing to make in the pursuit of customer satisfaction?

9.2.4   Inorganic Growth

A strategy of growth through acquisition implies a different line of exploration from a leadership risk perspective. It will be necessary to take a close look at the logic of a potential acquisition, what goals it serves to support, and how long it will take the investee company to realise the value of the acquisition. The investor/assessor will need to gather evidence that the organisation has the requisite collective skill and experience to execute acquisitions and then make them work and create value.

Clearly, it will be important to look at the management team's track record in successfully making acquisitions and negotiating the associated leadership challenges. It is important to determine how far they are aware of the inherent risks and problems around mergers and cultural integration that arise when one business acquires another.

In order to create real value, acquisitions must be fully supported by well-thought-through integration strategies. Acquisition strategies focus on the external commercial aspects of bringing organisations together, whereas integration strategies look at the internal organisational cooperation strategies. In order to ensure that acquisitions are a success, the organisation must be disciplined in thinking through critically how value will be created through the transaction. Once again, it is important to look at the investee company's history and experience in this area. It will be important to consider any previous acquisitions, their complexity, and how they fared before and after they were taken over.

9.2.5   Review of Existing Documentation

Depending on the degree of access in the context surrounding the leadership risk-mapping exercise, it may be possible to conduct a review of existing organisational documents. Documents such as those described below can be a fertile source of information about both the strategic and cultural dimension of the organisation. Examples of the types of documents which may be reviewed and the kind of information which they may yield are as follows.

Strategic Planning Documents

Strategic planning documents and presentations can provide useful insights into the strategic history of the organisation. Such documents will give a sense of how strategy has been formulated and to what degree of complexity, and also who has been involved in the strategic planning process. It can also be useful to compare such documents with the actual performance of the business as a means of gauging how effective the organisation is at strategic implementation.

Documents Relating to Change Initiatives

Documents such as presentations and mass emails may be available which relate to major change initiatives the organisation has embarked on previously. The tone and clarity of such documents can not only provide insights into the sophistication with which changes have been planned and managed, but also act as a cultural barometer. Again, it would be useful to establish how far the organisation was able to achieve the planned change in practice.

Human Resources Reports

It may be possible to view reports summarising trends and patterns relating to illness and absenteeism gathered by the human resources department. Increasing trends here, perhaps combined with increasing employee turnover, may provide an indication that the organisation is suffering from growing pains.

Customer Feedback

The extent to which the organisation gathers and considers customer feedback is in itself a useful piece of data. Where such data are available, the content of customer feedback reports can prove enlightening. Decline in customer satisfaction may also indicate that the organisation is overstretched.

Employee Satisfaction Surveys

Where an organisation conducts surveys of employee satisfaction this can yield extremely valuable information relating to leadership risk at an organisational level. The choice of questions used in such surveys can be salutary as an indication of what is valued and how willing the organisation is to look at itself reflectively. Responses from different parts of the organisation and the way these change over time can also be a useful indication of the level of morale in the organisation, the cultural climate, and the extent to which potential sources of resistance to change will exist.

9.2.6   Interviews and Focus Groups

Depending on the degree of access, it may be possible to conduct interviews or facilitate focus group discussions in order to promote understanding of the organisation from a top-down perspective. Individual interviews may, for example, be conducted with key stakeholders in the business such as non-executive directors, minority shareholders or even customers and suppliers. To gain a sense of the perspective of internal stakeholders from the employee population, it may also be possible and worthwhile to conduct individual or group discussions with individuals or groups from different areas of the business. As ever, careful preparation is required in developing a clear, well-chosen set of questions that will elicit insights most relevant to leadership risk. Examples of typical questions would include:

- Describe the things this business does really well.
- What would make this business more effective?
- If you could change one thing about this business, what would it be?
- The thing that causes most confusion/wastes the most time in this business is?
- When we have to make difficult decisions in this business what do we base our decisions on?
- What are the main ways in which this business has changed over time?
- What are the qualities which are most valued in this business?

9.2.7   Culture Surveys

As well as looking at existing employee satisfaction surveys which may have been conducted in the past, the scope of the leadership risk assessment may also allow the administration of an organisational questionnaire specifically designed to gather information relevant to leadership risk. Such surveys can be administered online and, as with other components of a leadership risk assessment, it is important that respondents are properly briefed about the purpose and reassured as to the confidentiality of their responses. The style, length and content of such surveys will be dictated by the scope and purpose of the assessment in question. It is important that every item is clear and that the overall questionnaire is not too onerous to complete. The scope of the current chapter precludes a detailed examination of all possible questions which could be included in such a survey. In the previous chapter we began to look at what data are relevant to understanding culture as it exists on different levels. For the purpose of the current discussion it may be useful to consider the kind of questions which may be included in such a survey that might yield information about what is happening on the deepest and least tangible level of culture within the organisation. At this level, culture relates to the collective impact of people's unconscious beliefs and assumptions about the organisation. Stan Lees, whose work was introduced in the previous chapter, suggests that questions about the following areas can be useful as a means of testing the basic assumptions upon which the culture of an organisation is based:

- What drives the business?
- How is governance practised?
- Over what timeframe do people think?
- How is the business oriented in relation to its market?
- How tight or generous are margins?
- Where does power lie in the business?
- How does the business manage risk and uncertainty?
- How does the business view and treat its human capital?
- How does the business treat reels and mavericks?
- Is the business more oriented towards teams or individuals?
- How does the reward system work?
- How much diversity is there within the business?

Individual responses to such questions can be compared and combined to build an overall picture.

9.3   DATA FROM OTHER LEVELS OF ASSESSMENT – THE 'BOTTOM-UP' VIEW

9.3.1   Individual Assessment Interviews

In building a picture of leadership risks at an organisational level, significant indications can be gleaned from data gathered during assessment of key individuals and the leadership team. Clearly, the interviews which form part of these assessments can shed light on organisational themes and it may be appropriate to include organisational questions in the interview guide, such as:

- 'Thinking about the strategy going forward, which elements do you think will pose the biggest challenge and why?'
- 'What makes this business successful and what gets in the way of success?'
- 'What are the main priorities for the business?'
- 'What are the key changes people expect to see in the business going forward? How well do you think they will deal with these?'
- 'What could hamper success in the future?'

Beyond these specific questions, a number of the data sources used to assess on an individual and team level may reflect broader organisational issues when viewed together. Some examples include the following.

9.3.2 Information on Skills and Competences

The overall competency profile of the senior executive population, as indicated by the multi-rater feedback and interviews, will provide a barometer of the level of talent which the organisation has at its disposal. It may, for example, emerge that the population tend to have the same skills profile – all sharing similar strengths and development needs. Any systemic gaps in competency need to be evaluated in light of the strategy and the leadership journey ahead. It may also be worth exploring the landscape of overall strengths and weaknesses in light of the values promoted in the organisation; what is valued and not valued.

9.3.3 Psychological Preferences

It can be useful to consolidate the outputs from the psychometric instruments to assess whether there are any particular psychological preferences which run through the management population. If the preferences are too skewed overall, this can suggest a leadership risk for the organisation. For example, if the senior leaders share a preference for thinking in very concrete and practical terms, this may cause problems if the strategy requires them to think more creatively. It may also be the case that the dominant psychological preferences amongst the senior population have an impact on the wider culture. For example, it is not uncommon to find that senior leaders in private equity-backed businesses share a preference for approaching their work in a fast-pace and energetic manner. This can be very positive in maintaining a high level of productivity, but it does carry the risk that they may move too quickly and leave others – lower down in the organisation – behind.

9.3.4 Motivation

As discussed previously, motivation is particularly difficult to assess and in practice will probably only register on the leadership risk map where the motivations of one or two senior individuals are significantly at odds with the business agenda. A potential leadership risk at an organisational level could arise from a situation where the senior leadership population appears to have widely different motivations.

9.3.5 Clarity of Team Purpose

Clearly, if it emerges that the senior team do not have a clear, shared sense of purpose, this has profound implications for the organisation and represents a leadership risk in the broadest sense.

9.3.6 Team Processes and Governance

From an organisational perspective, it is important that the processes and governance procedures in place within the senior team reflect the needs of the wider organisation. One important area to explore is the interface between the senior team and the organisation itself in terms of how information flows from the organisation to the team and how the team interacts with the organisation in order to achieve the results it desires.

9.3.7 Team Dynamics

Within the context of team dynamics, it is also useful to consider the dynamic which exists between the senior team and the wider organisation. Discussion with, and observation of, the senior team should provide an indication of how healthy and open the interaction is between the team and the wider organisation, or whether there is a disconnect.

9.4 SUMMARY

- Conducting a leadership risk assessment at an organisational level involves looking at data related to the organisation as a whole ('top down') as well as more detailed data from the individual- and team-level assessments ('bottom up').

- It is also possible to categorise organisational data in terms of what it reveals about the organisation's potential to deliver strategy as well as sources of possible interference.
- Central to the top-down perspective is the behavioural strategic review which involves working through the planned strategy in order to determine the key leadership risks and milestones which it implies. Different strategies will have different leadership risk implications. A further top-down technique is to review existing organisational documentation such as previous strategic planning documents, documents relating to change initiatives, human resource documents, customer feedback and employer satisfaction surveys.
- Top-down information can also be gathered by specially conducted one-to-one interviews or focus group discussions.
- Depending on the context and timing of the review, it may also be possible to conduct cultural surveys. These can be especially useful in highlighting some of the less tangible, unconscious aspects of organisational culture.
- Data from the bottom-up perspective could include the results of questions asked about the organisation during individual assessment interviews.
- A further perspective on the organisation can be gained by looking at the combined picture emerging from the competencies, psychological traits, motivational state and team picture which emerges from the other levels of analysis in the leadership risk assessment.

REFERENCE

Treacy, M. and Wiersema, F. 1996. *The Discipline of Market Leaders*, Perseus Books.

10

The Review Phase

Risks associated with the review phase of the leadership risk-mapping framework include:

- Insufficient time is given to the review, with the result that important findings are overlooked.
- The underlying causes of findings are not explored sufficiently – disproportionate 'blame' is placed on individuals and insufficient account is taken of the importance of the surrounding context.
- Conclusions are reached on the basis of single findings and are not properly tested through triangulation with data from other sources.
- Themes and issues are considered in isolation and not related back to the big picture.
- Themes from individual and team level are insufficiently framed in terms of the wider organisation or implications.

10.1 INTRODUCTION

The final two phases of the leadership risk-mapping framework are extremely important, as it is during these phases that the results of the review are translated into plans and actions which will maximise the opportunities for the business to succeed and reach a satisfactory exit. Clearly, the conclusions which are drawn in the review phase (discussed in this chapter) and the actions which are formulated in the address phase (described in Chapter 11) depend on the data which are gathered earlier on in the process. In practice, the review and assess stages of the framework mark the beginning of an ongoing cycle which can be repeated through to the exit point and beyond. The review phase involves using all the data gathered as a basis for reflection upon where the business is in respect to the various dimensions of leadership. On the basis of the business and leadership agenda to come, the data are linked into themes, conclusions are draw and priorities are set. On the basis of this actions are defined (in the address phase). It is then important that the various themes and issues are actively tracked over time and

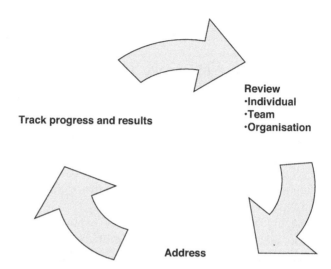

Review
·Individual
·Team
·Organisation

Track progress and results

Address

Figure 10.1   Cycle of ongoing leadership risk review

the action plans fine-tuned and revised if necessary, meaning that there will be an ongoing cycle of further data gathering, reviewing and action planning. See Figure 10.1.

This chapter sets out the approach to adopt when reviewing data gathered in the assess phase and highlights some of the considerations which need to be borne in mind to ensure that the picture which emerges and the conclusions which are drawn are clear and accurate. We begin the chapter by revisiting the four quadrants of awareness and setting out for each quadrant the relevant factors to consider in order to ensure that the data is properly reviewed and the findings can then be properly addressed. We return to the three levels of analysis covered in earlier chapters (individual, team and organisational assessment) and, for each of these, suggest how the results may be presented in a way that facilitates effective review.

10.2   CONSIDERATIONS IN THE FOUR QUADRANTS OF AWARENESS

10.2.1   Investee's Outer World

The framework necessitates the gathering of data from multiple sources and it is important that all data gathered are brought together and presented in a clear and accessible manner, which can be linked both back to the original plan and to any summaries which are prepared as a basis for future action. By the time the review phase of the process is reached, members of the leadership team will have invested considerable time and patience and will be as curious as the investor to see the results, if not more so. Careful consideration therefore needs to be given as to how best to present the findings to members of the investee leadership team. Even if the review was conducted as part of pre-deal due diligence, and will therefore have been very much under the ownership of the investor, the investee team will still feel a degree of entitlement to see the results. If the review was conducted on an existing portfolio business but by the investor rather than the investee, it is even more important to be transparent in sharing the results. However well planned and detailed the review has been, it can only ever represent a summary picture of the underlying complex reality – the reality of the investee team, the investor, the relationship between the two and the business. The investee leadership team therefore has a role to play in interpreting the results, and for that reason the review process should be as collaborative as possible. The investor should be careful not simply to present the investee management team with their own conclusions. It should also be remembered that this is a highly personal and sensitive exercise, so great care should be taken to preserve the confidentiality of the results and access to the data gathered and the ultimate outcomes of the review should be tightly controlled. Due recognition and thanks need to be given to the wider group of interviewees and feedback respondents (for example, those who participated in 360-degree feedback exercises). There will be an expectation on the part of wider stakeholder groups that they will be given at least some information relating to the findings of the review. Again, it may be best to collaborate with the investee management team in deciding what key messages need to be communicated and how best to do this. As we will describe below, individual members of the investee leadership team should receive personal feedback on their part of the assessment and be given the necessary space and resources to help them process the feedback and translate it into a suitable development plan. Similarly, at a team and organisational level, it is important that time is set aside to review and 'digest' the findings and that all those affected are properly involved.

10.2.2   Investee's Inner World

As mentioned previously, undergoing a leadership risk-mapping assessment is a highly personal experience and it is important to remain sensitive to the feelings and reactions of the investee management team. The underlying tone and approach used to present feedback and work through the review should, as far as possible, convey support and reassurance. As far as possible, the process should be participative and constructive. Some members of the investee management team may be confronted with surprising and perhaps unwelcome messages. It is critical here to recognise that individuals require time and space to process personal feedback before they reach a point when they can translate those insights into a development plan. The review and address phase of the leadership risk-mapping process offers a real opportunity to reinforce and strengthen the relationship between the investee management team and the investor, as long as the feedback is managed in a positive and constructive way, in the spirit of an exercise which is ultimately in everyone's best interest as it aims to benefit the business.

10.2.3   Investor's Outer World

After careful planning and data gathering, it is important that the investor sets aside sufficient time and devotes proper attention to reviewing the results. All of the data needs to be reviewed in the light of the high-level priorities which come from the business agenda. The importance of emerging themes and issues needs to be evaluated in light of their potential impact on the business. In reviewing the results, the investor must cultivate the discipline of constantly asking 'how will this help on the journey to exit?' and 'how could this issue threaten to destroy value in the business?'

In interpreting the results, the investor should think in terms of both current implications and also the future of the business and the leadership journey through to exit. It is this discipline which makes it possible for the framework to provide a clear, hierarchical map of the population of leadership risks which confront the business.

10.2.4   Investor's Inner World

In working through the findings the investor should guard against being overly influenced or distracted by any biases or misconceptions they have. As described in earlier chapters, some private equity investors are innately sceptical about psychological data or information which is not easily quantifiable. It is, therefore, important that the investor approaches all the data with an open mind in order to realise the full benefit which data from multiple sources enable in producing a rich, multi-dimensional picture. The investor should also be willing to revisit their instincts and hypotheses, which may have been developed on the basis of gut feeling. In some instances, the review will confirm what the investor already thought, but it is also important that the investor is willing to recognise instances where their innate gut feelings actually prove to be unfounded.

10.3   THE REVIEW PROCESS

At the heart of the review phase is a process of reflection and digestion of the data gathered, in which both the investor and the investee should participate. We underlined the importance of resisting the temptation to begin interpreting and evaluating data before the assess phase is complete, but once all data have been gathered the review can commence. To ensure the review is conducted in a thorough and disciplined manner, the gathered data for each level of leadership should be explored from the perspective of the terms from the 'inner game' formula introduced earlier (potential and interference), and also considered in terms of both the current and future needs of the business. The core questions can be summarised in the following table:

	Present	Future
Potential	Does the business have the necessary leadership capability to meet its current needs?	Does the business have the necessary leadership capability to meet its future needs, given the critical path to exit?
Interference	Are there any factors or issues which get in the way of the business fully accessing and realising the leadership potential which exists within it?	Are there any factors or issues which could, in the future, get in the way of the business fully accessing and realising the leadership potential which exists within it?

Any findings which fall within the left-hand 'present' column will form the basis of the immediate development agenda, which will have to be implemented to bring the business on track. Issues in the right-hand 'future' column indicate the issues which will need to be addressed on the route to exit. We will explore these questions in more depth below in terms of how they might be applied to the various levels of analysis. The review should be as collaborative as possible. An iterative approach may be taken in order to allow key themes to emerge and crystallise as follows:

Step 1 Compile all data gathered
Step 2 If possible, discuss and review it with the people who have been assessed
Step 3 Identify and document the high-level priority implications

10.3.1 Individual-level Review

Probably the most important factor to consider when reviewing leadership risk data at an individual level is that the individual under review should be able to participate in the process as much as possible. In order for the review to be successful in raising awareness of key leadership risks and establishing a focused development plan, it is vital that the individual concerned is given time and space to reflect on their emerging profile and have a say in its interpretation. Not only will close collaboration and discussion with the individual help with the interpretation of the data and locate emerging themes properly in their context, but giving the individual a sense of active involvement and a degree of control will help to reinforce a sense that the review is positive and constructive and so increase the individual's motivation to address the areas identified and reach their development objectives.

Clearly, a key factor in determining how much the individual members of the leadership can become involved will be the timing and nature of the leadership risk assessment. If the exercise is being done as part of pre-deal management due diligence, then it is likely that significantly less direct discussion and review will be possible. At the other extreme, if the review is being done on an existing portfolio business and it is the investee management team who have commissioned the review, then it can be expected that a good deal of 'digestion' of the results will have already been done before the investor even sees the results.

In the former scenario, where joint review with the leadership team members is not feasible a disciplined approach to the review of the data is needed, based on questions such as:

- 'How do the various pieces of data fit together?'
- 'What conclusions can be drawn and based on what evidence (there should be more than one piece of supporting evidence)?'
- 'What issues will have the biggest impact on the business and are therefore most important?'

- 'Are all the issues identified attributable solely to the individual concerned or are there any underlying organisational themes?'

10.3.2   Presenting the Data

Before the data can be fed back to the individual leaders, it is important that they are presented in a format which can be readily interpreted and which facilitates the raising of awareness. Data from the multi-rater feedback exercise and individual interviews should be reviewed together in order to build up a picture of where the individual is on each of the key competencies identified in the planning phase. It is particularly useful to express this in narrative form and for each competency to list out areas of strength and areas of possible concern. If appropriate, it may be useful to indicate the level of competence quantitatively – perhaps on a scale of 1 to 5. However, this should not be seen as a substitute for narrative description. To build an effective development plan it is important for the individual to have rich and meaningful feedback data to work with. It is common to present data on psychological preferences in the form of expert-generated computer reports. If these are to be used, it is important that the report in question is presented in everyday language with a minimum of jargon. A more time-consuming but user-friendly alternative is to have a personalised profile, specially written for each individual (for example, by a corporate psychologist). Once the assessment data have been compiled into an accessible format they can then be discussed with the individual in a personal feedback session. We have discussed earlier that receiving personalised feedback is a potentially highly sensitive experience. If a third-party firm was used to conduct parts of the assessment, it can be a good idea to arrange for the initial feedback discussion to be completed by a representative of that firm. This approach has a number of advantages:

- Providing feedback through a neutral third party will make the feedback discussion feel less 'loaded' and so hopefully make for a more open discussion.
- Individuals from such third-party suppliers will be experienced in facilitating feedback discussions and so will be able to conduct the feedback review in a way which enables the individual to process the feedback effectively and derive the maximum benefit from it in terms of future development.

- Having the opportunity to participate in a feedback discussion where the individual has the option of raising certain issues in confidence increases the chances of bringing any underlying contextual issues to the surface.

A typical feedback discussion will last between one and three hours depending on the amount of data to be discussed. The person giving the feedback should begin the session with a reminder of the wider process which has generated the feedback, the overall objectives of the process and the specific objectives of the feedback session. The individual will be encouraged to raise any questions or concerns they have and to highlight any further objectives they may have for the session. The person giving the feedback and the individual will then walk through the various pieces of data bit by bit, highlighting themes along the way, identifying any connections and thinking about the implications by viewing the feedback messages within the context of the leadership agenda and the individual's personal objectives.

It is important to recognise that it takes time to process personal feedback, particularly if it contains surprising or unpleasant information. The individual's initial reaction may be quite emotional and they may experience feelings of shock or anger. It is unrealistic to expect that the feedback will be fully processed during the course of one feedback session. Therefore, once the data have been discussed with the individual the best approach is for them to reflect further, possibly for a week or so, before fully formulating their personal development plan. In some instances, where a third-party consultant is used to facilitate the individual feedback process, it may be useful for this individual to facilitate a second, three-way, feedback meeting involving the individual and their line manager during which the draft development plan is reviewed in more depth. As mentioned above, the important thing is that the individual feels they have ownership of the development plan. If the investor is tempted to formulate individual development agendas themselves and then attempt to impose these on the individual members of the leadership team, this is likely to limit the chances of the development really taking hold.

Once each individual has formulated a personal development plan, this can be 'validated' by comparing it with the data gathered in the assessment phase and the high-level leadership risk-mapping objectives defined in the planning phase to ensure that it appropriately addresses the underlying themes and risks. If any gaps are identified these should be addressed by further discussion with the individual. Such discussions should be conducted in the spirit of arriving at a development plan which will ultimately help the business to achieve its objectives and which is therefore in everyone's best interests.

10.3.3   Team-level Review

Again, the starting point for reviewing data from the team-level assessment is to sift through data from the various sources and bring out the key themes and messages. For example, responses to questions on the team gathered from the various individual interviews can be compared in order to establish how far team members have a shared vision of what the team's purpose is and see whether they provide consistent accounts of how the team manages key processes. Where team effectiveness questionnaires have been used, the results of these can be consolidated to calculate the team's average score on the various dimensions of team performance which have been identified. It can also be useful here to gauge the range of responses and to see whether different stakeholder groups tend to have different perspectives on the team. Themes from the multi-rater feedback should be compared with the results of observing the team in action. The results of the review can then be presented in a narrative form, where each key theme is described in a paragraph of text with reference to the supporting documentation. A next step may be to review the team summary document with the team leader, and this discussion can be used to decide how best the data can be explored with the team as a whole.

One approach here is for the team to participate in a 24-hour developmental planning workshop. Again, it may be best that this is facilitated by a third party to create a 'safe space' in which the data can be explored in a constructive manner. A rough agenda for the workshop would be to begin in the late afternoon or evening of day one with the team reviewing the data. The second day then begins with a review of the key business objectives and strategy, and the remainder of day two is devoted to a facilitated discussion by the team of what the developmental priorities are, based on the data and business agenda. By the afternoon of day two it should have been possible to formulate a high-level draft development plan for the team.

10.3.4   Organisational Review

In some ways the review of data gathered at an organisational level is the most abstract of all and it may be worth considering this level of analysis once the individual and team review and feedback process is complete, because only then will all the 'bottom-up' data be available. The results of the various discussions and document reviews which will have been conducted relating to the organisation's history of formulating strategy, and planning and implementing change, should be summarised in narrative form, including an overall conclusion about the following:

- The level of change which the organisation will have to negotiate on the path to exit.
- What evidence exists to suggest that it can manage this.
- Which areas will come under most pressure and which areas require careful monitoring for signs of 'growing pains'.

It will also be useful to compile a narrative description of the key facets of the organisational culture, with a clear indication of any potential sources of cultural resistance to change which have been identified.

Depending on the emerging picture it may then be appropriate to discuss some or all of the organisational risk map with the chief executive of the business and possibly members of the senior team to test the conclusions, put them into context and think about next steps.

10.4   REPORT FORMAT

The leadership risk-mapping report should present clear-cut conclusions and interpret the key findings in terms which can be easily related to other pieces of information relevant to the business. The report should begin with a cogent and succinct summary of key findings and conclusions, preferably captured on one or two pages. A hierarchical structure is useful as this enables the reader to drill down into increasing levels of depth, so as to understand the audit trail which underpins key findings.

Overall then, the tests of a good leadership risk-mapping report are that it is:

- Clear – no jargon and easy to understand.
- Relevant – it can easily be located within the wider business context.
- Useful – the implications and recommendations are clear.
- Balanced – in providing both summary conclusions and detail where it is needed.

A leadership risk summary report will often consist of the following elements:

- Executive summary
- Business-level risk assessment
- Individual-level assessment
- Team-level assessment
- Appendices.

10.4.1 Executive Summary

The executive summary provides an overview of high-level conclusions. Although the conclusions here cannot be stated with the same level of certainty as, for example, a traditional kind of risk assessment, they should highlight the key leadership-related issues which could impact the business agenda in the short to medium term. If the review is being conducted as part of pre-deal management due diligence then it may be appropriate to include a summary statement of whether, in the overall opinion of the assessor, the management team has the capacity to deliver the proposed business plan and which areas require attention. It should also include key points in relation to:

- Overall points of strength.
- Areas requiring attention.
- Conclusions and high-priority recommendations.

10.4.2 Body of the Report

The body of the report should then describe the findings from the different elements of the review and in each section explain what process was used and what was found. If the review has embraced all three of the dimensions described earlier in this book, it could be expected to contain the following.

Business-level Assessment (see also Appendices VIII and IX)

Business- and organisational-level risks can be usefully summarised on one page in the form of a risk map. This can then be broken down into greater detail, perhaps in the form of a table describing key risks, their potential impact, possible mitigating factors and recommendations to address them. The description of each risk should be clearly linked to elements of the strategy and the changes they imply.

The business level of the assessment should be documented in a way which enables the high-level leadership risks to be incorporated into the wider landscape of other business risks. Following from the discussion at the very start of this book, given the complexity and uncertainty surrounding leadership risk it is not feasible to think in terms of 'probability', but key leadership which appears to have a reasonable chance of manifesting can be charted in terms of the timescale over which this might happen (for example, the next three months, the next year or beyond the next year) and the potential impact it may have on the business.

Graphics can be useful in bringing the overall risk landscape to life, as Figures 10.2 and 10.3 illustrate.

In the examples shown, the likely timescale during which the issue may manifest is indicated by its proximity to the centre of the chart and the potential impact is shown by its shade. Figure 10.2 shows an example of a high-level leadership risk map, where each segment equates to a

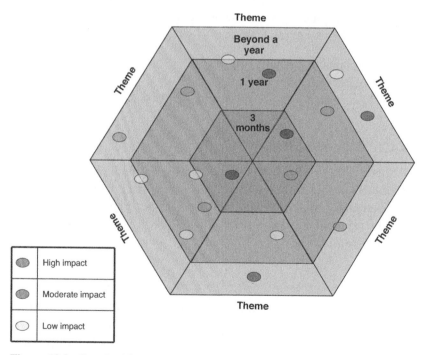

Figure 10.2   Sample risk map

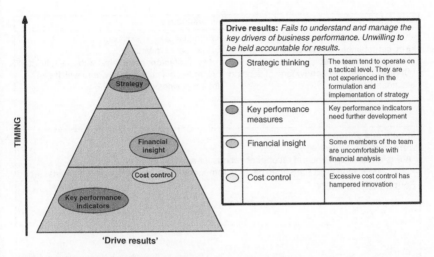

Figure 10.3   Sample risk map – detail

particular leadership theme. Figure 10.3 illustrates how such a summary chart may be broken down to describe the underlying issues within each leadership theme.

Individual-level Assessment (see also Appendices I, II and III)

The individual section should contain a summary for each individual member of the management team, showing high-level strengths and weaknesses and suggestions for development. It may also include a benchmark summary showing how the individual compares with the wider management population, measured against the same parameters they were assessed against. The detailed results from the psychometric tests and reference interviews can be provided in an appendix. See Figure 10.4.

Team-level Assessment (see also Appendices IV, V, VI and VII)

The team-level assessment should describe the key aspects of the team dynamics, possibly also presented in the form of team maps (see the example in Appendix VI). It should also contain comments on the implications of dynamics for achieving results and explain which aspects of the team will need to be focused on, in order to deliver the strategic agenda.

Some investors find it useful to combine the results of the individual assessments of team member competencies to provide an overview of

Strengths	Weaknesses
•Key contributions to the business •Key contributions to the team •Main points of impact •Competencies and behaviours influencing business success	•Potential gaps in skills set •Potential derailers •Key risk factors associated with the individual •Competencies and behaviours which can inhibit business success

Impact and actions
•Key strengths to leverage
•Areas for development and recommendations for action
•Other suggestions/recommendations (e.g. remuneration policy, performance targets, etc.)

Benchmark summary

Mr Blue – Benchmark Summary	Below Par		On Par		Above Par
Managing Interpersonal Relationships			⬭		
Drive Results				⬭	
Building a team		⬭			
Adapt and change				⬭	
Leadership Expertise			⬭		

Figure 10.4   Sample individual summary

the team which shows how members compare with each other, as in Figure 10.5.

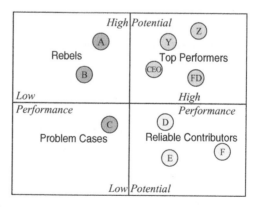

Figure 10.5   Sample team summary map

10.5 SUMMARY

- During the review phase it is important that all data gathered are considered in a balanced and methodical manner.
- The review and address phases of the process can be seen as first steps in an ongoing cycle through which action plans are fine-tuned in the light of experience.

- As far as possible, members of the leadership team who have been assessed during the process need to be actively involved in the review phase in order to ensure the results are put into context.
- It is important to bear in mind that receiving feedback can be a sensitive and uncomfortable experience for the individuals who have been assessed and it may take them some time to 'process' the feedback and translate it into a development plan.
- In the review phase, the data gathered should be considered in terms of what they reveals about the potential of the organisation and its leaders to deliver what is needed now and in the future as well as current and possible future sources of interference.
- Data gathered from individual assessments should be consolidated and put into a clear and coherent format so that they can be reviewed in a personal feedback session with the individual concerned.
- It may be better if individual feedback is provided by a neutral third party and in confidence.
- Following the feedback session the individual should ideally generate their own personal development plan which should then be discussed with their line manager or the investor.
- Team-level data should also be synthesised to produce a clear narrative report summarising the key themes and conclusions. This can then be reviewed and explored by the team in order to establish a team development plan.
- The organisational-level review is perhaps the most abstract. At this level it is important to reach a conclusion about the organisation's capacity to manage the change ahead, highlighting any particular pressure points and describing any potential sources of resistance to change.
- The organisational-level analysis can then be discussed with the chief executive and possibly the senior leadership team.
- The results of the leadership risk-mapping process can be presented in a hierarchical written report with an executive summary showing the key conclusions, sections covering each level of analysis and appendices containing the detailed data.

11

The Address Phase

Risks associated with the address phase of the leadership risk-mapping framework include:

- There is a failure to translate findings into proper development plans.
- The development plans which are produced do not lead to lasting changes which benefit the business.
- There is a failure to establish clear development priorities based on the broader business agenda.
- The development agenda is skewed so that there is disproportionate focus on one dimension and not enough attention given to others.
- The development agenda is too focused on short-term issues and fails to address the full strategic journey.

11.1 INTRODUCTION

Unlike the previous three phases of the framework, the address phase is open-ended and effectively continues until exit is achieved. As mentioned in the last chapter, once the data have been gathered on each level of analysis, this should mark the beginning of an ongoing cycle of review, planning, action and then further review. Addressing the issues identified through the process is arguably the most significant element of the framework because, unless the leadership risk-mapping assessment translates into appropriate action and development, it will have been of only theoretical interest. For the purposes of this book, this stage is perhaps the most difficult to describe because the precise means of addressing the issues which emerge depend on what those issues are and the context. It would be misleading to imply that there are universal approaches which will address leadership risk across different businesses – taking adequate account of context is key.

When considering how to address the findings of the leadership risk review it is important to remember that the individuals involved will already be extremely busy and probably working under considerable pressure. It is also important to recognise that personal and organisational change can be a difficult process and that the development

agenda from the leadership risk-assessment process may involve changing habits and patterns of behaviour which may have been in place for
a considerable period of time and may have been entirely legitimate
and appropriate when they were first established. In view of this it is
worth considering some basic ground rules during the assess phase, for
example:

- Be selective – as far as individual- and team-level development is
  concerned, the development agenda should not include more than
  three or four issues to focus on at any one time.
- Identify priorities – development plans should address those factors
  which have the biggest impact on the business or which represent the
  biggest threat.
- Link to outcomes – development activities should be clearly linked
  to outcomes which in turn should be connected to business performance.
- Be realistic – development objectives should be based on a realistic
  appreciation of what can be achieved within what timescale.
- Act quickly – if difficult people decisions have to be made then it is
  best that this is done as soon as possible and that such decisions are
  properly explained to all those affected.
- Track progress – as mentioned in previous chapters, leadership risk
  mapping is an ongoing process so development plans must be framed
  in terms of clear milestones against which progress can be measured
  and in light of which plans can be adapted.

In this chapter we will consider how to address the findings arising
from a leadership risk-mapping exercise, looking at each of the three
levels of analysis (individual, team and organisational) around which
the framework is based. For each of these levels we will set out the main
factors to consider under each of the four quadrants of awareness.

11.2   ADDRESSING LEADERSHIP RISK AT AN INDIVIDUAL LEVEL

11.2.1   Investee's Outer Perspective

From this perspective the aim is to establish a clear development plan for
each individual member of the management team. As mentioned above,
it is a good idea for the development plan to focus on what a successful
outcome will look like and that there are clear links between this outcome
and the ultimate performance of the business. If a development issue

relates to a particular kind of leadership behaviour then a useful starting point may be to reflect on what other people will have noticed if the issue in question were to be addressed successfully. Where multi-rater feedback has been gathered in the assess phase, this may provide useful clues as to what the individual should stop doing, start doing, keep doing or do differently.

In terms of identifying priorities, it is usually best to begin with issues which will have an impact on current performance and move onto development needs which affect the future needs of the business once the current needs have been met. The different aspects of individual leaders covered during the assessment phase may imply different approaches when it comes to establishing a development plan. Where development needs exist in the area of key competencies it is important to be pragmatic and realistic when deciding how to address these. Again, the best starting point is to think in terms of the ultimate outcome. Although learning to perform a particular competency more effectively may seem the most obvious way forward, this may not represent the best use of an individual's time and energy. It may also be worthwhile exploring alternative approaches such as drawing on other competencies, where the individual is already seen as being effective or even reassigning responsibility or reallocating resources so that the outcome is achieved by another means. Where a development need is seen to stem from a particular personality trait, development will often centre on the individual placing increased awareness on that aspect of their personality and the impact it has on others and using this awareness to manage themselves in a way which produces the desired outcome. Where leadership risks are more attributable to the motivations of the individual, this should be addressed through careful and sensible discussion between the individual and the investor in order to arrive at a clear set of expectations and priorities. The individual's personal plan should be clearly documented with a description of each development issue, its impact on the business, a description of a successful outcome and a list of actions which the individual will take in order to achieve the desired outcome. Careful consideration should be given to what further resources may need to be drawn upon in order to implement their plan effectively.

In some instances it may be useful for the individual to draw on the support of an external coach to ensure that they maintain focus and momentum in addressing their development agenda.

Typically, an individual coaching intervention will entail regular one-on-one sessions with a coach over the course of several months so an agenda can be developed and worked through. The coach will act as a sounding board, supporting the individual to identify and implement changes in his or her work situation.

To ensure that coaching yields as much benefit as possible, both to the individual and to the organisation as a means of mitigating leadership risk, care should be taken in selecting a coach. In their book *Business Coaching: Achieving Practical Results through Effective Engagement*, Peter Shaw and Robin Linnecar state that a good coach must be able to understand:

- The role and dynamics of the organisation.
- The person and personality of the client.
- The situation the client is in.
- The stage of learning the client is at.
- The process of the client relationship.

Shaw and Linnecar suggest that a good coach must demonstrate the following qualities:

- Being grounded and having deep self-awareness.
- Not seeking to achieve one's own ambitions through others.
- Holding unconditional positive regard for the client.

11.2.2 Investee's Inner Perspective

In order to maximise the chances that development initiatives take hold and translate into business benefits, it is important that the members of the investee leadership team feel as if they have ownership of their development agenda. It is, therefore, very important that they do not feel that the development has been imposed on them or that they have a feeling of being controlled. Again, having an open, collaborative development planning process will help here. Ideally, most, if not all, elements of an individual's personal development plan should be generated by them on the basis of the picture emerging from the review, the awareness and insights that this yields, and a consideration of these insights in light of the business context. Working through the development agenda can be a challenging process, and some individuals may find it useful to have confidential coaching support in doing this.

11.2.3 Investor's Outer Perspective

The investor will need to build a clear picture of how any gaps identified in the leadership risk map will be addressed through the development agenda. It should be possible to break these down into clear outcomes and expectations. The investor should also identify opportunities where they could provide support to the individuals as they work through their development plans. They may, for example, be able to offer advice and insights from experience with other portfolio businesses, and in some instances it may be appropriate to bring in resources from elsewhere in their portfolio. As mentioned earlier, leadership risk mapping should be seen as the beginning of a process and it is, therefore, important that there are mechanisms in place that will ensure the development plans established as part of the exercise remain on the agenda and in the awareness of the leadership team and do not get forgotten. Identifying and actively tracking milestones on the development journey can help here. However, it is also important to allow some flexibility in the plans so that they can be fine-tuned in the light of experience and can be adapted to reflect any changes in the business agenda with the wider environment.

11.2.4   Investor's Inner Perspective

It is important that the investor remains aware of their own emotional reactions to the results of the leadership risk-mapping exercise. It may, for example, be that the profile of the key individual that emerges from the leadership risk-mapping exercise is different from what the investor had expected. If the investment is being conducted on an existing portfolio business it may emerge that certain leaders do not possess the strengths they appeared to have when the investment was made. This may provoke a range of feelings on the part of the investor – such as anger, frustration, disappointment or impatience – so it is important that they channel their energy positively and focus on how to move from where the business is to where it needs to be without dwelling unnecessarily on the past.

11.3   ADDRESSING LEADERSHIP RISK AT A TEAM LEVEL

11.3.1   Investee's Outer Perspective

To address leadership risk at a team level it is necessary to start by considering the overall clarity of purpose which the team has and how well this is linked to the business. Unless the team has a clear sense of purpose, any development activities focusing on other areas may be misdirected. If, therefore, the team-level assessment suggests that the team is not clear about its purpose this must be addressed and resolved as a matter of priority. The approach here will involve providing an opportunity to consider the data gathered during the assess phase and discuss this with the support of the investor and possibly a third-party facilitator in light of the strategic plan and the desired exit scenario in order to establish a shared vision.

The overall purpose of the team can then form a solid foundation for planning further development as it will represent a point of reference against which the structure, processes and governance policy of the team can be compared in order to identify gaps. Once gaps have been highlighted, the team can then identify actions to close them. Particular care should be taken if the team assessment has revealed a gap in the composition of the team. A possible remedy here will be to introduce one or more new members to the team, but such a process should be handled with tact and sensitivity. Where new individuals are to be introduced into a pre-existing, well-established team it is important that there is a clear integration plan which will enable them to manage the transition from outsider to team member as smoothly as possible. If the team is under pressure there may be a temptation to overlook the integration agenda for new team members, but to do this may cause problems going forward. Factors to consider in order to ensure a smooth integration of new team members include the following:

- Ensure the new team member fits the team as closely as possible, not just in terms of the knowledge and competencies which they bring but also in terms of their mindset and outlook.
- Ensure that the role of the new team member has been properly defined and clear expectations set.
- There should be a high level of shared determination among the other team members for the new person to succeed in the role so that they will be supported in achieving their objectives.
- Any lingering political issues should, as far as possible, be dealt with before the person comes on board.
- The process for providing the new team member with clear, honest and timely feedback should also be in place.
- Finally, it is essential that the new member of the team is provided with a thorough briefing about both the business and the cultural context which they are moving into.

It may be that a smoother and quicker integration is achievable if the new team member is promoted from elsewhere in the organisation, rather than being recruited from outside.

11.3.2   Investee's Inner Perspective

Where the results of the assessment phase suggest that team dynamics represent a problem, it is best if the team is given the latitude to address this internally. Again, drawing on the support of a third-party facilitator can help in the process. If it emerges that trust is lacking in the team this should be addressed as a matter of priority. Here, the very act of raising awareness that trust is an issue and acknowledging the ways that different members of the team feel can be a good starting point. It is also important that team dynamics are considered if a new member is to be brought in. Particular care should be taken if the new team member is a representative of the investor's business or if the investor has recommended their appointment. In this case there is a danger that the new individual may be perceived as a potential threat and treated with suspicion, which could impede the integration process.

On an inner level it could be that the team assessment reveals or awakens a number of unspoken concerns within the team, so it is important that teams give themselves sufficient time and space to work through these issues.

11.3.3   Investor's Outer Perspective

From the investor's point of view, it is important to be as supportive and collaborative as possible when addressing team-level assessment. There may be a temptation to impose solutions on the team which have worked in other investee businesses. However, even if the investor is able to perceive a clear solution to team-level development needs, it is important that time is invested to obtain the full buy-in of the team. In working with the team in order to establish a focused development plan. The investor should strive to support them in the process of identifying their own solutions whilst maintaining an appropriate level of challenge to ensure that the development plan will achieve the desired outcomes.

11.3.4   Investee's Inner Perspective

As with the assessment phase, it is important that the investor remains sensitive to the dynamic which exists between them and the leadership team. Again, it is important for the investor to cultivate a high level of self-awareness around the emotions they associate with the team to ensure that these do not impair the relationship. Emotions such as frustration or disappointment should be tempered, so that the investor's attention and energy can be directed constructively in order to support the investee team in working through a development plan which will help them bring the business to where they and the investor want it to be.

11.4   ADDRESSING LEADERSHIP RISK AT AN ORGANISATIONAL LEVEL

11.4.1   Investee's Outer Perspective

Addressing leadership risk at an organisational level often involves establishing systems and processes to track the development which needs to take place at an individual and team level. The exercise should have provided a clear sense of the skills and behaviours which the business will need on its route to exit and therefore which dimensions of leadership behaviour should receive the most attention. These insights can then form the basis for ongoing activities, such as:

- Performance management
- Objective setting
- Defining incentives
- Talent management
- Succession planning
- Recruitment and integration
- Establishing and managing a talent pool.

The above processes all exist at a formal level. It may also be necessary to refine or redirect change management initiatives in light of what the review has revealed about the culture of the organisation.

11.4.2   The Inner Perspective of Investor and Investee

It is important to recognise that leadership risk assessment exposes a depth of organisational reality which no amount of financial analysis would reveal. Where the assessment is conducted as part of pre-deal management due diligence, to a certain extent both parties involved in the deal will have created what is, in effect, a shared fantasy or idealised vision of what things will look like after the deal has been completed. Everyone will have been on their 'best behaviour', making every effort to make a positive impression and to paint a compelling picture of how successful the business will be. And on an inner level, all parties involved will have unspoken doubts and fears. The reality is that some aspects of the collective idealised vision may come true, but others may not. No matter how thoroughly everyone involved has prepared themselves for what happens once the deal becomes reality, things will not all go to plan. Through the leadership risk-mapping exercise, the investor may be forced to confront some of the gaps which exist between the initial 'fantasy' and the reality, and it is important that any feelings which this may provoke do not cloud the process of establishing a constructive organisational development plan.

11.5 SUMMARY

- In deciding how best to address the findings of the leadership risk-mapping exercise it is important to be as discriminating as possible in order to ensure that focus is placed on the highest-priority areas and that these are properly linked to business outcomes.
- In individual development planning it is best to begin by focusing on the outcome which is desired and to work back from this. Development issues relating to current performance should be given a higher priority than those relating to what the business will need going forwards.
- It should not be assumed that the best solution is always to learn to perform a competency more effectively. Other strategies may include reallocating responsibilities or substituting other approaches in which the individual is more adept.
- Individuals may benefit from having the support of a personal coach as they work through their development plan.
- Individuals will feel more ownership of their development agenda if they have been actively involved in defining it, so it is important that development activities are not imposed.
- At a team level the first priority is to ensure that there is clarity of purpose. Once a clear sense of purpose has been established, other team development activities can be planned in relation to this.
- If it is deemed necessary to introduce new team members, care should be taken to ensure that they are integrated as quickly and as efficiently as possible. The impact of introducing new team members on team dynamics should not be underestimated.

- At an organisational level some of the activities arising from the leadership risk assessment will relate to the establishment of systems and processes to monitor progress going forward.
- Insights into organisational culture should be reflected in change management plans.
- At an organisational level both the investor and the investee will have to come to terms with the reality of the business and the way in which this may differ from the idealised view they may have held before the deal took place.

REFERENCE

Shaw, P. and Linnecar, R. 2007. *Business Coaching: Achieving Practical Results Through Effective Engagement*, Capstone.

12

Third-party Service Providers and their Approaches

Risks associated with the involvement of third-party service providers in leadership risk assessment include:

- External suppliers focus more on their approach than the wider context, so that the results they produce cannot easily be translated into action.
- The objectivity of third-party suppliers is compromised as they aim to sell other services.
- The style or approach of a supplier chosen by the investor causes unnecessary disruption to the investee management team, which impairs the relationship between investor and investee.
- The 'chemistry' between the investor, the investee and the supplier does not work.
- Third-party suppliers use a rigid, pre-defined framework which does not fit the specific context of the business.
- Conducting the entire leadership risk assessment 'in-house' means that perspective and objectivity are lost.

12.1 INTRODUCTION

The framework described in the previous chapters provides a roadmap for investors and investee management teams, which will guide them through the process of understanding and addressing leadership risk so as to maximise the chances of creating value. If a leadership risk-mapping exercise is conducted, then the overall ownership of this process must rest with either the investor or investee management team. However, owning the process and actually conducting the review or elements of it are not the same thing, so it is possible, and even likely, that at some stage in the process it will be necessary to call on the support of third-party service providers. Given the sensitivity and complexity associated with the assessment of leadership risk, the decision as to whether to use third-party suppliers and, if so, which ones requires considerable care. The aim of this chapter is to set out some of the key considerations which need to be borne in mind when making decisions in this area.

At several points in the preceding chapters we have acknowledged the high level of skill and experience which many investors have in the assessment of management teams. The instinctive 'gut feel' which many investors draw upon when evaluating the leaders of their investee businesses is often a useful barometer, and the techniques described in the foregoing chapters are intended to be seen as a means of complimenting or validating the investor's gut feel rather than replacing it. However, there are several reasons why an investor may decide not to carry out the full leadership risk assessment themselves, but instead commission a third-party provider to do some of the in-depth assessment and feedback. One factor to consider here is the time it takes to conduct the review. Investors are normally confronted with a punishing and very busy schedule and have to be selective about how they spend their time. Given the high opportunity cost of the investor's time and the time-consuming nature of leadership risk mapping, in many cases it may be felt that it is more efficient to have the work done by a third party. A second factor to consider is that, as we have shown through the four quadrants of awareness model referred to in previous chapters, the investor represents a dynamic component in the overall leadership risk landscape and is therefore 'part of the equation'. The clarity of insight around the areas of leadership risk may therefore be clouded if the investor conducts the assessment whilst simultaneously being part of that which is being assessed. Involvement of a more independent third party will help to address this. The use of gut feel may also be an issue. Although the investor's instincts can be a useful guide, they can also be a source of bias. If the assessment is conducted in an entirely objective manner by a more independent third party, the findings can then be used to confirm or challenge opinions based on instinct. A final factor to consider is the degree of professional expertise required to conduct some steps in the leadership risk-mapping framework. As discussed at the beginning of this book, investors have considerable expertise in conducting complex financial and commercial analysis but do not usually have the same depth of expertise in the assessment of leaders. Moreover, the use of some techniques, such as psychological analysis, requires that the person conducting the assessment has professional accreditation. It may be that the investor concludes that leadership risk is so central to their business that it is worth establishing a dedicated in-house team, and this would address many of the points set out above. However, for investors who do not follow this option and, indeed, for dedicated in-house leadership risk assessment teams, the current chapter is designed to provide a guide to the most important factors to consider when drawing on the support of third-party suppliers. We begin the chapter by framing the key considerations within the four quadrants of awareness model. We then set out the different approaches to leadership assessment which are adopted by the main suppliers in the market and give indications of the advantages and disadvantages of each.

12.2 CONSIDERATIONS IN THE FOUR QUADRANTS OF AWARENESS

12.2.1 Investee's Outer Perspective

From the outer perspective of the investee management team, it is important that any third-party suppliers involved have the necessary credibility to conduct the review. This will stem in part from their level of experience in having conducted similar assignments and whether they have the right professional credentials. In terms of knowledge and insight, it is particularly important that whoever conducts the assessment has an appropriate balance between professional expertise in the assessment of individuals, teams and organisations and a depth of commercial insight and understanding which will ensure that they appreciate the business context. From the outer perspective of the investee team being assessed, it is also important that the approach used causes the minimum disturbance and makes the very best use of whatever time is available. For leadership risk assessments which are conducted on existing portfolio businesses, it may be that the investee leadership team pay for the assessment themselves or it could be that the investor recharges part of the cost. In either instance, it is important that the quality of service provided is seen to represent good value for money. Given the high stakes associated with leadership risk and the extent to which value creation and destruction hinges on the performance of the leadership team, it would be a false economy simply to choose the cheapest supplier. Nonetheless, the quality of service and the results delivered should clearly demonstrate value added. Finally, whether the assessment is commissioned by the investor or the investee, it is important from the point of view of the investee management team, that the provider is seen to operate in an independent and objective manner so that the emerging picture of the leadership team is as clear and true as possible.

12.2.2   Investee's Inner Perspective

As we have pointed out in previous chapters, leadership assessment is a personal and potentially threatening experience for its subjects. For members of the investee leadership team to fully buy into, and cooperate with, the process and reveal themselves in sufficient detail to enable an objective assessment, it is vital that whoever conducts the review is able to gain their trust. A further factor to consider, therefore, is whether a third-party supplier has the necessary inter-personal skills which, in combination with the professional credibility described above, will enable them to gain the trust and respect of the members of the investee management team.

12.2.3   Investor's Outer Perspective

If the investor has primary responsibility for commissioning the leadership risk assessment (as will almost always be the case if the review is being conducted as part of pre-deal due diligence and will often be the case for reviews of existing portfolio businesses), then they will also be concerned that any potential supplier is able to demonstrate high standards of quality and professionalism. Investors will be accustomed to working with lawyers, accountants, bankers and other professionals and there is no reason why they should compromise the standards they expect from these other suppliers. The investor will also be particularly keen to ensure that any potential supplier is able to frame their offering within the wider business context and is able to describe their approach and explain their findings in terms of their business implications. It will help, therefore, if the supplier is able to present what they are doing in a clear manner using the same language as the investor and without resorting to jargon. Particularly in cases where the review is conducted as part of pre-deal management due diligence and the investor is in the early stages of forming a relationship with the investee management team, they will be concerned that any third-party suppliers who are commissioned to assess the investee management team reflect well on the investor and act as a good 'ambassador'. If anything about the third-party supplier presents the investor in a bad light, this could have significant repercussions and may jeopardise the deal.

12.2.4   Investor's Inner Perspective

As we have described previously, some aspects of leadership risk mapping will take the investor outside their normal sphere of understanding, and this experience of moving into 'unknown territory' may not be a comfortable one. It is, therefore, especially important that any third-party provider is able to imbue confidence in the investor and provide a sense of reassurance. There should be an appropriate culture fit between the investor and the supplier, and the chemistry and rapport should work well in order to ensure that the investor feels fully confident in trusting a supplier to effectively act as their representative.

12.3   THIRD-PARTY SUPPLIERS AND THEIR APPROACHES

Having set out some of the high-level considerations which may influence the decision about which third-party supplier to use, we will now review some of the main types of suppliers who provide relevant services. The purpose of the current discussion is to describe the approach which will typically be adopted by the following four categories of supplier:

1. Executive search firms
2. Corporate psychologists
3. Strategic consultancies
4. Specialist 'boutique' firms.

Most providers of leadership risk-assessment services will fall into one of these categories and, although the approaches overlap to a certain extent, it is possible to distinguish between the different offerings and identify advantages and disadvantages for each.

12.3.1   Executive Search Firms

In recent years a number of executive search firms have developed a service line which relates to the assessment of management teams. Several of these firms have dedicated teams who work for private equity investors and provide support in conducting management due diligence and portfolio reviews. Unsurprisingly, the approach commonly adopted by executive search firms closely mirrors the core skills which they apply in other parts of their business. Their reviews, therefore, typically centre on in-depth interviews combined with some feedback gathering and the occasional use of psychometrics. In the course of a typical year, an executive search professional may meet and interview dozens or even hundreds of executives; this helps to make them adept at assessing on an individual level, and gives them a depth of insight into how well a person may match up with a particular role. A typical interview with a recruitment specialist may, therefore, often centre on the competency-based approach which we have described in earlier chapters.

Advantages of Executive Search Firms

Search consultants can be expected to be very experienced at assessing senior people. They are often effective at 'benchmarking' executives against a senior population, even if this is against an informal gauge based upon their experience and judgement. Experienced search consultants will have assessed many senior executives, and have an internalised calibration of what a high-performing executive looks like. They may be willing to assign a numerical rating to individuals. While the numbers are no more than relative indicators of largely subjective judgements, investors appreciate an element of quantitative analysis. Search consultants should also have a clear view of what they are looking for, as they are accustomed to comparing individuals with role specifications. Close contact with their clients should also ensure they are quickly able to build a sound understanding of the overall culture and climate of a client organisation and its constituent departments and teams.

Disadvantages of Search Firms

Given the core business of executive search firms, clients may question the objectivity of their leadership risk assessments. If their assessment arrives at a conclusion which would then provide them with a lucrative search assignment, this could put them and their client in an awkward position. Also, the ability of search consultants to appreciate the financial and commercial dimensions of the business in depth may not be strong. One of the arguments in favour of the approach set out in this book is the importance of integrating information on leadership effectively with other dimensions of business and putting their findings into context. The investor may therefore have to establish for themselves how to locate the results of such a review in a wider business context.

12.3.2   Corporate Psychologists

Another category of service providers who have begun to work with investors are corporate or business psychologists. Such firms typically have a pre-defined framework for conducting individual- and team-level assessments, which often entail the subjects of the assessment going through a battery of psychometric tests. The emphasis here will be on building a detailed picture of the different dimensions of personality.

Advantages of Psychologists

Consultancies with psychological approaches are likely to be more rigorous and systematic in testing and are therefore arguably more 'scientific' in their approach. Such approaches make it easier to compare test results with a valid norm group, which may be useful to the client. Moreover, a more in-depth psychological assessment can do more to get below the surface and thus increase the chances of identifying 'false positives' – executives who make a strong impression but who have underlying weaknesses. Moreover, experienced organisational psychologists are more attuned to the subtle links between different aspects of individual psychology and business performance. They may also have more sophisticated tools for conducting analysis on a team level.

Disadvantages of Psychologists

Psychometric testing can be time-consuming and so can try the patience of some people. A management team may feel over-tested, or even insulted by psychometric testing. An overtly psychologically based form of questioning can also be perceived as threatening. For testing to be credible in the eyes of management, it must have demonstrable links with performance. Whilst some psychologists have strong commercial awareness, many lack a deeper understanding of business and a sense of the nature of the investment. They may not fully appreciate the time pressures involved, and the enormous pressure that executives can be under. Another criticism is that they sometimes make excessive use of psychological jargon in their reports, making the findings difficult to interpret.

12.3.3   Strategic Consultancies

A number of firms who have traditionally provided strategic advice and worked with investors to conduct commercial due diligence have expanded their offering to include management due diligence. Again, it is common for the assessments offered by these firms to centre on a standard approach, although the emphasis of the approaches provided by different firms varies from the more psychological (some employ psychologists) to the more competency-based. For such suppliers the review of the management team is seen as being supplementary to the wider, commercial assessment of the business.

Advantages of Strategists

Strategists are likely to have a very good understanding of the business side, and should be better able to integrate the findings of management due diligence with other forms of due diligence if the review is performed pre-deal. Users may find it convenient to source the different forms of due diligence from one provider, especially if there is a long-established relationship between the two organisations. Compared with psychologists, strategic consultants are likely to have more business credibility, and potentially a more pragmatic approach. They are more likely to understand the role that the psychological dimension plays in the wider commercial picture, and to focus on the tests that highlight abilities which are most relevant.

Disadvantages of Strategists

Leadership assessment is not the core business of strategic management consultancies, so they may not necessarily be able to integrate the two sides. They may be using this service as a loss leader, using it to sell other services. They are also likely to be less experienced in testing teams than the specialist psychometric providers, for example. Moreover, in the case of a large consultancy such as one of the major accounting firms, the approach may be somewhat rigid and programmatic. There may be an institutional preference for frameworks and processes, and a tendency to go for a pre-existing approach. This has the advantage of consistency, but the consultancies may lack flexibility, and may lack awareness of the context of the deal. A private equity deal can be intricate and have specific strategic nuances, so the standard frameworks and reports of large firms may not pick up on the right areas.

12.3.4   Specialist or Boutique Suppliers

The three categories of suppliers described above each have a core business which in some way overlaps with leadership risk assessment and entails the application of some relevant skills, but it is not a core service offering. The final category of supplier, on the other hand, makes leadership risk assessment more of a core offering. Service providers in this category may have a background in one of the types of organisation described above, but have then set up smaller, more specialist businesses and defined an approach which is more closely tailored to the specific needs of investors. Such suppliers are more likely to field a range of experts from different disciplines and have a more flexible approach which can be adapted to the specific need of the investor.

Advantages of Specialists

Such specialists will be dedicated to leadership risk assessment, so there will be no other agendas and no competing priorities and no other business opportunity is being sought on the back of the review they offer. Specialists will have a much higher level of familiarity with, and exposure to, the world of private equity investments. They are more likely to assess in depth, and at different levels: at the individual level, the team and the wider culture of the organisation. Specialists are also likely to make a greater investment in the development of dedicated tools and frameworks and more investment in relevant training and development on their part.

Disadvantages of Specialists

As this is a relatively new field it may be difficult to check track records. No single model is applied, which can accentuate an already difficult selection process. A specialist provider will typically have a background in one of the areas described above, so may be prone to some of the disadvantages listed there. Some of the larger firms may also be rather programmatic. A balance must be struck between a systematic approach and the flexibility required for tailoring approaches to the circumstances. For example, a provider may have a framework for effective entrepreneurs that defines five elements of high performance in private equity deals, or a model for team effectiveness. These become the elements which are assessed and presented in the report, but in the particular context other factors could be key. Or the model may involve assessing individuals, whereas the important challenge in the context is to obtain a good balance in the team.

In summarising the position of the various suppliers, it can be useful to locate them in relation to one another in terms of how far they strike a

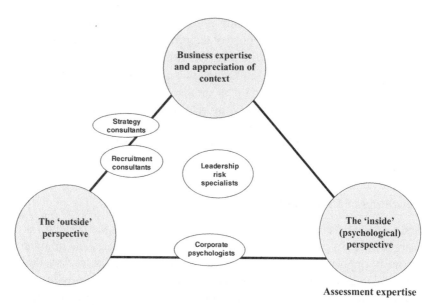

Figure 12.1 Balance of perspective of third-party providers

balance between the three perspectives which we have drawn on in the leadership risk-mapping framework (the 'inner' or 'self' perspective, the 'outer' or 'other' perspective, and the context). The rough positions of the four supplier groups described above can be seen in Figure 12.1.

12.4   IDENTIFYING POTENTIAL SUPPLIERS

One way to identify potential suppliers is through personal networks and via word of mouth. The obvious place to start is with trusted sources, such as former colleagues or professional advisors (lawyers, bankers and accountants). Most of the bigger suppliers will have websites. Some of their experts will speak at conferences or seminars and may write thought leadership pieces in the media.

Another crucial factor is the degree of objectivity which the supplier brings to the assignment. There may be a risk, for example if a recruitment consultant is involved, that they perceive the management due diligence review as a way of generating recruitment business. Although many recruitment consultants are extremely adept at accessing management teams and benchmarking them against the wider management population, it is vital to structure the review process so as to ensure an impartial view. If the prospective supplier is a strategic consultancy, it is important to establish that they are not using management due diligence assignments as a route into organisations with the primary objective of selling other services or products.

It is also important that the firm has the necessary resources available to conduct the review. However, it is important not to be overly influenced just because the firm is large. In practice, a single expert may provide a much better review than a team of less-qualified individuals.

A further important consideration is the experience of the organisation and the individuals who will conduct the review. As previously discussed, many new suppliers have entered the market in recent years. Thus it is important to probe the organisation around how many similar reviews they have previously carried out by asking them about which other private equity firms they have worked for, the size of the deals they have worked on, and the sectors which they have previously been involved in. From this, the investor can gain a sense of how experienced they are. If possible, other existing clients should be consulted.

The way in which the engagement team presents itself and how its members interact reveal a lot. A harmonious team in which each person upholds a common approach will probably inspire more trust than individuals who do not seem to work well together.

It is also essential to meet the individuals who will actually be conducting the review and ascertain their level of technical qualification, understanding of business and finance, and possibly most importantly of all, to judge their interpersonal skills and how they are likely to come across to the management team.

It will also be important to gain an understanding of the supplier's underlying philosophy and how they will approach the review. The critical point here is to look at how well the framework used to evaluate management matches the requirements of the investor, and how likely it is to yield findings which answer their key questions and address the most significant management-related risks which will impact the investee business. The investor will want to gauge how flexible the supplier is, and whether they have a standard solution which they sell to everyone. It is also worthwhile finding out which tools they use – for example, which psychometric tests they tend to use and why they rely on them, as well as exploring any specific approaches they use.

As well as meeting with prospective suppliers, it is important to review samples of their work. These will normally take the form of sample reports from which all confidential material has been removed.

The quality and clarity of the writing and the vocabulary used will give an overall impression of the level of professionalism of each supplier. A reliance on psychological jargon will be a negative, as will a lack of references to the business context surrounding the assessment. As suggested above, it is standard practice to take references and, if possible, to speak not only to other private equity investors who have worked with the supplier but also members of management teams they may have assessed in the past.

12.5 SUMMARY

- Although the overall ownership of the leadership risk-mapping process must remain with either the investor or the investee management team, it can be useful to draw on the support of third-party suppliers for some elements of the process.
- Given the sensitivities of the process, however, it is important that the choice of supplier is given careful consideration. Factors to consider when selecting a prospective supplier include:
  - Checking their level of skill and experience.
  - Exploring the extent to which they specialise in this service to be delivered.
  - Understanding their approach.
- Different suppliers will be able to provide support in different elements of the process and approaches may vary. For each category of supplier and approach, there are both advantages and disadvantages.
- Executive search firms may provide support in conducting individual assessments or gathering multi-rater feedback. They have the advantage of having met a broad population of senior executives, but the provision of this kind of service is not central to their business and some investors may question their objectivity.
- Corporate psychologists may also provide support in assessing at each level, particularly when it comes to those parts of the framework relating to core, psychological preferences. The advantage of corporate psychologists is that they bring expertise in the area of individual psychology. However, they may struggle to put their findings into context and if their procedures are too abstract, they may alienate the people whom they are assessing.
- Consultancy firms may also provide support, particularly in assessing leadership risk at an organisational level. Such firms are likely to be well placed to understand the business context but in most cases this

type of service will not be their core business and they may be rather rigid in their approach.

- The final category are firms which specialise in advising on qualitative risk assessment, such as leadership risk mapping. Such firms are likely to bring a greater breadth and depth of expertise, although some may be rather programmatic in their approach.
- One way to gain an overview of the population of possible suppliers is to evaluate them on in two dimensions: the degree to which they are able to bring business insight and, on the other hand, their level of expertise in assessing senior leadership populations.
- In deciding which firm or firms to work with, it is also important to get a feel for the chemistry and culture, and undertake appropriate quality checks and gain references from other firms who have used them.

Appendix Overview

'Leadership Risk: A Guide for Private Equity and Strategic Investors'

LIST OF APPENDICES
(SAMPLE QUESTIONNAIRES AND OUTPUTS)

INDIVIDUAL-LEVEL ASSESSMENT

- Appendix I – Sample Individual Leadership Risk Summary
- Appendix II – Sample Detailed Individual Leadership Risk Profile Report
- Appendix III – Sample Individual 360° Feedback Report

TEAM-LEVEL ASSESSMENT

- Appendix IV – Sample Team Leadership Risk Summary Map
- Appendix V – Sample Team Effectiveness Questionnaire
- Appendix VI – Sample Team Dynamics Summary Maps
- Appendix VII – Sample Aggregate Team Competency Summary

ORGANISATIONAL-LEVEL ASSESSMENT

- Appendix VIII – Sample Organisational Leadership Risk Summary Map
- Appendix IX – Sample Culture Risk Map

Appendix I
Sample Individual Leadership Risk Summary

'Mr X'

Key strengths

- Intellectually sharp – quick mind
- Strong analytical abilities
- Keen commercial insight
- Highly focused on delivery
- Driven and energetic
- Dedicated and hard-working
- Resilient under pressure
- Sets high standards
- Grounded, confident manner
- Clear focus on customer needs
- Confident decision-maker
- Sets clear direction
- Perseveres in the face of obstacles

Points of possible concern

- More tactical than strategic
- Prone to perfectionism
- May outpace others
- Struggles to let go and delegate
- Prone to impatience
- Narrow leadership repertoire
- Resistant to input from others
- May overlook signs of burnout in others
- Can appear aloof and distant
- Not an active listener

Benchmark Summary

Competency	Well Below Par	Below Par	On Par	Above Par	Well Above Par
Delivery – Focuses on the achievement of exceptional results				●	
Leadership – Creates a clear compelling vision, empowers others and manages stakeholder relationships			●		
Judgement – Makes effective decisions based on clear insight into business and people			●		
Resilience – Is driven and determined and works effectively under pressure				●	
Personal Impact – Interacts and communicates confidently and effectively with others		●			

Sample Detailed Individual Leadership Risk Profile Report

'Mr X'

Confidential
Date

This report is a professional interpretation of the leadership characteristics of Mr X, which has been compiled as part of the leadership risk-mapping assessment of XYZ Ltd. The purpose of the report is to provide insights into Mr X's profile, which can be used to inform his approach as a member of the senior leadership team of XYZ Ltd.

Structure

The report consists of a 'Profile' which looks at the following areas:

- Delivery
- Leadership
- Judgement
- Resilience
- Personal impact.

For each area, relevant scores from Mr X's psychometric profile have been included.

The final section highlights 'Conclusions' which summarise Mr X's key strengths and development needs [*See example in Appendix I*]

This report should be reviewed together with Mr X's Personal Feedback Report, which contains feedback from others relating to the five areas listed above [*See example in Appendix III*].

Delivery

He is a vigorous and determined individual who maintains a very clear sense of what he wants to achieve. He makes delivery a top priority and takes a pride in achieving spectacular results and exceeding his targets. He spends time building a clear understanding of what customers need and expect and dedicates himself to meeting their requirements. He actively involves himself to ensure that any problems are adequately addressed. However, some feel that he sometimes gets too involved in the detail and a more patient, measured approach would improve overall efficiency. He is extremely hard-working and drives himself and others sometimes very close to the limits of capacity. He appreciates the importance of remaining sensitive to signs of burnout. His strong focus on delivery and hard-working nature leave him little time for reflection and, to maintain success in the medium to long term, it is important that he makes space to think strategically about how market demands will change over time. He sets high standards for himself and others and carefully monitors quality at every stage. He recognises that he runs the risk of being a perfectionist and strives to challenge himself to ensure that his expectations around quality are realistic.

		Very Low	Low	Average	High	Very High	
Goal-oriented	Complacent						Ambitious
Assertiveness	Passive						Assertive
Activity level	Inactive						Fast-paced
Sense of duty	Unreliable						Dependable
Anger	Patient						Irritable

Leadership

He is comfortable taking charge and acting decisively and prefers to be in control. He has a clear sense of what he wants to achieve and paints a clear picture for his team about how they fit into the overall vision and what he expects from them. His drive and determination provide impetus to those around him, although his serious-minded outlook limits the extent to which he enthuses others. He recognises that he is, by nature, rather tough-minded and unsympathetic and he tends to adopt a directive style of leadership. Whilst this leaves no one in any doubt as to where the business is heading and what is required of them, the style limits the extent to which some members of the team feel really engaged. To maintain success and ensure that the business grows as expected, he needs to broaden his repertoire of leadership styles and become more supportive and collaborative at times. His high appetite for control means that delegation can be a challenge for him. He strives to let go and empower others, although this remains an ongoing development need and is particularly difficult for him when problems arise and deadlines are in jeopardy. By nature he is rather cautious and suspicious and, although he appreciates some of the suggestions which have been made by the General Partners, he is more comfortable when he feels he has the latitude to manage things himself without outside input. Going forward, it is important for him to be more proactive in asking for advice and support as the business grows in complexity.

		Very Low		Low		Average		High		Very High	
Modesty	Self-accepting											Modest
Trust	Suspicious											Trusting
Willingness to experiment	Narrow range											Versatile
Enthusiasm	Serious											Exuberant
Compliance	Stubborn											Cooperative
Sympathy	Tough-minded											Compassionate

Judgement

He likes to work through problems in a logical, systematic fashion. He gathers data carefully in order to build a clear picture on which to base his decisions. Although capable of using intuition, this is not his preferred style. He is likely to become uncomfortable if he is required to make significant decisions in situations where data is ambiguous or incomplete. His preference for logical thinking and rigorous analysis can mean that he overlooks some of the more subtle, qualitative dimensions of problems and he may not always adequately consider the people implications of his decisions. He is intellectually sharp and is quick to identify key priorities. His quick mind and strong focus on delivery mean that he is keen to work through problems quickly and he may close down group discussions before they have run their course. He is confident in his judgement and takes full responsibility for his decisions. He recognises that, going forward, it will be necessary for him to participate more in group decision-making, which will involve him engaging with team members whose thinking styles are different from his own.

		Very Low		Low		Average		High		Very High	
Imagination	Concrete										Abstract
Self-belief	Unsure										Self-confident
Open to ideas	Narrow focus										Open-minded
Deliberation	Hasty										Cautious
Orderliness	Unmethodical										Orderly

Resilience

He is an active, energetic individual who injects pace into all that he does. Once he has identified an objective, he pursues it with a strong sense of purpose and perseveres in the face of obstacles with a sense of determination. He has a deep-seated work ethic and is willing to make personal sacrifices in order to achieve his ambitions. His preference to move quickly and drive things forward at all times means that he may run the risk of leaving others behind. Given the challenging targets facing the business, it is also important that he remains sensitive to signs of burnout and fatigue in his team. He is not prone to stress and is able to remain calm and clear-thinking even when the pressure mounts significantly. His skills in planning and organisation help to ensure that he is well prepared and this reduces unnecessary pressure, although there can be times when his processes are overly rigid, making it difficult to adapt.

		Very Low	Low	Average	High	Very High	
Anxiety	Calm						Anxious
Stress vulnerability	Clear-thinking						Panicky
Open to emotions	Limited emotional range						Wide-ranging emotions
Self-discipline	Distractible						Persevering
Moodiness	Hopeful						Pessimistic

Personal impact

He is a confident, grounded individual who speaks in a focused and business-like manner. His style when dealing with others conveys energy and determination. Although he is passionate and animated when talking about the business, he is less comfortable when it comes to engaging with others on a more social level and he prefers to keep others at arm's length. He can appear rather intense and more junior staff from within the business may feel somewhat cautious when approaching him. His tendency is to focus more on the content of his communications rather than the impact which he is having on others. Although he is careful to manage his style when dealing with customers in order to maintain an effective relationship, he is less sensitive to the needs and feelings of those from within his own organisation. To some he may appear aloof or even arrogant. He does not always invest sufficient time to listen carefully to others and he can be too quick to decide what it is they are going to say. He tends to influence others in the business through force of personality and his position of authority. Moving forwards, it is important that he cultivates a wider range of influencing skills. Here, a willingness to express greater warmth and invest more time in building rapport could help.

		Very Low		Low		Average		High		Very High		
Self-assurance	Self-assured											Self-conscious
Warmth	Reserved											Friendly
Consideration for others	Self-absorbed											Helpful
Outgoingness	Introverted											Gregarious
Open to values	Conventional											Unconventional

Appendix III

Sample Individual 360°
Feedback Report[1]

'Mr X'

PERSONAL FEEDBACK REPORT

USING YOUR REPORT

Your feedback report is based on the questionnaires completed by you and your colleagues. Ratings were elicited on separate statements that together contribute to a group of competency areas. The questionnaire items are individual behaviours and the competencies are headings under which groups of behaviours are clustered. Each statement was rated on a numerical scale and these ratings reflect how you were perceived to demonstrate each of the behaviours by your colleagues (and yourself).

Remember as you look at your report that all of the ratings are based upon perceptions, which tend to be more subjective than objective. Try to interpret the ratings of your colleagues within the context of your work, and the way you may appear to others. Don't try and work out who has said what – this is difficult and misleading.

You will find the following sections in the report. A brief outline is given below, followed by a more detailed description of each of the outputs on the next pages.

Cluster Profile

This consists of bar charts summarising your ratings, broken down by cluster. The charts summarise your ratings according to respondent type (self, peer, and so forth). For respondent *groups* the ratings are averaged

---

[1] Report format reproduced with the kind permission of Compass 360.

across that group. Note that any ratings for 'Not Applicable' are simply excluded from the averaging process.

Gap Analysis

This set of tables allows you to compare your own ratings with those of other respondents. The report shows for each statement the difference between your self rating and each of the respondent groups' rating. A positive gap means that others have rated the statement higher than your self rating. A negative gap indicates that others have rated the statement lower than your self rating. The table displays rank orders of your greatest *blind spots* (biggest negative gaps) and your greatest *unrecognised strengths* (biggest positive gaps).

Response Range

This will tell you what ratings you got from each of your respondents, but without naming them. The distribution of ratings is given only in terms of respondent type.

Competencies in Rank Order

This section shows all of the competencies you requested feedback on, arranged in order of the average of others' ratings.

Behaviours in Rank Order

This section shows all of the behaviours you requested feedback on, arranged in order of the average of others' ratings.

Scatterchart

Showing the correlations between your own ratings for each competency and the ratings from all others.

Comments

This section shows the comments your respondents have made.

CLUSTER PROFILE

Cluster Profile Chart

These bar charts present your 360-degree feedback for each of the competency clusters. Each one of the clusters is made up from several competencies which are in turn described by the behaviour statements that form the items of the questionnaire.

The ratings for each statement were collated and then assembled under their competency headings, then under their cluster headings and then averaged. These averages are presented here as bar charts – you can use these charts to compare the impression people have of you for each of the high-level cluster areas. Averages are presented for each respondent group. The rating scale goes from 1–5, where 1 is *Never* and 5 is *Always*.

The thin line below some of the bars shows the range of responses that went to make up the main bar above it. This helps to show the range of different opinions among respondents.

The cluster average score shows the average of all rater scores (including self) for each cluster.

As well as rating yourself, you were rated by 3 direct reports, 3 peers, 1 line manager and 3 investors.

DELIVERY

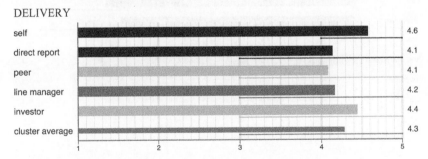

LEADERSHIP

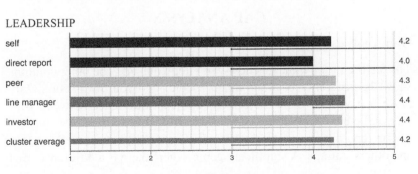

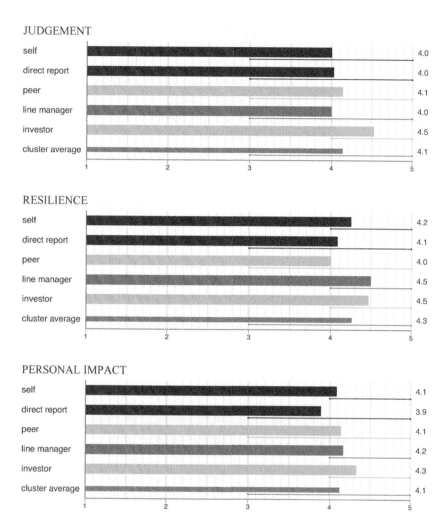

JUDGEMENT

self		4.0
direct report		4.0
peer		4.1
line manager		4.0
investor		4.5
cluster average		4.1

RESILIENCE

self		4.2
direct report		4.1
peer		4.0
line manager		4.5
investor		4.5
cluster average		4.3

PERSONAL IMPACT

self		4.1
direct report		3.9
peer		4.1
line manager		4.2
investor		4.3
cluster average		4.1

GAP ANALYSIS

Gap Analysis Report

The 'self' column indicates how you rated yourself. The other columns show the difference between others' scores and your own score. Only those behaviours where there is a significant difference between your own and others' ratings are shown.

The report shows up to sixteen significant gaps between your rating and others' ratings. A significant gap is where there is a difference of at least 0.5 points between your *self* rating and others' ratings. The positive gaps and negative gaps represent your most significant unrecognised strengths and blind-spots, respectively.

Behaviour	Self	Direct report	Peer	Line manager	Investor	All
Sets clear expectations when delegating	3.0	+1.7	+1.3	+2.0	+1.3	+1.6
Builds trust so that team members are comfortable admitting mistakes and can learn from them	3.0	+1.3	+1.3	+1.0	+1.7	+1.3
Collaborates effectively where possible and appropriate	3.0	+1.0	+1.3	+1.0	+1.7	+1.2
Able to analyse from multiple perspectives	3.0	+1.0	+1.0	+1.0	+1.7	+1.2
Conveys a sense of purpose and mission that enthuses others	4.0	=0.0	+0.7	+1.0	+0.7	+0.6
Sensitive to signs that pressure may be getting to others	4.0	+0.3	=0.0	+1.0	+0.7	+0.5
Is driven and goal oriented – persists in the face of obstacles	4.0	=0.0	+0.3	+1.0	+0.7	+0.5
Able to remain calm and clear-thinking under pressure	4.0	+0.3	−0.3	+1.0	+0.7	+0.4
Thinks strategically to develop new products and services which are driven by, and aligned with, future customer needs	5.0	−0.7	−1.3	=0.0	−1.0	−0.8
Able to adapt to rapidly changing situations and priorities	5.0	−1.0	−1.0	−1.0	−0.7	−0.9
Ensures decisions and activities are aligned with the investor's long-term plans	5.0	−1.0	−0.7	−1.0	−1.0	−0.9

(Continued)

Behaviour	Self	Direct report	Peer	Line manager	Investor	All
Allocates resources and effort according to strategic priorities	5.0	−1.0	−1.0	−1.0	−0.7	−0.9
Invests time and energy to develop further as a leader	5.0	−0.7	−1.3	−1.0	−0.7	−0.9
Anticipates questions and issues where the investor will require information and explanations	5.0	−1.3	−0.7	−1.0	−1.0	−1.0
Has a balanced understanding of themself and others	5.0	−1.3	−1.0	−1.0	−0.7	−1.0
Projects a relentless sense of urgency and purpose	5.0	−1.3	−1.0	−1.0	−0.7	−1.0

RESPONSE RANGE

Response Range Table

This is simply a table showing how people have used the rating scale for each of the questionnaire statements.

You can use this information to identify where you may be coming across differently to different colleagues or groups of colleagues.

For example, an average rating of 2, say, in one of the bar charts could have been awarded because everybody agreed to rate you as a 2. But it may be that one person has rated you as a 5, and 3 others have given you a 1. The average is the same, but that average can hide the polarisation of perceptions. It may be useful for you to consider why it is that different people have different opinions of your behaviour.

In the following table, an S shows where you rated yourself, a D shows where a direct report rated you, a P shows where a peer rated you, an L shows where a line manager rated you and an I shows where an investor rated you.

Delivery

Behaviour	1	2	3	4	5
GOAL ORIENTATION					
Allocates resources and effort according to strategic priorities			P	DDD PLI I	SPI
Initiates changes to organisational structure, systems and processes which match strategic objectives			P	SDD DPL II	PI
Thinks strategically to develop new products and services which are driven by, and aligned with, future customer needs			PP	DDI II	SDP L
Shows absolute commitment to the achievement of business goals			DPI	SDD PLI	PI
Monitors progress to ensure delivery			DP	SDD PLI I	PI
Sticks with issues until they are properly resolved			PL	SDD DP	PI I
QUALITY					
Sets high performance standards for self and others				DPL II	SDD PPI
Able to sustain a high level of productivity whilst maintaining quality			P	SDD PLI	DPI I
Willing to do whatever it takes to deliver at the highest possible standards			DP	DDI I	SPP LI
Establishes processes and procedures for managing quality			P	DDP L	SDP III
Invests time to understand and exceed customer expectations			P	DPL I	SDD PII
Strives to share best practice across the business				DDP PII	SDP LI

Leadership

Behaviour	1	2	3	4	5
SETTING DIRECTION					
Shares a clear and compelling vision for the future of the business			PI	DDI I	SDP PL

(Continued)

Behaviour	1	2	3	4	5
Ensures that everyone is driven and focused				DDD PPI	SPL I
Conveys a sense of purpose and mission that enthuses others			D	SDP I	DPP LI I
Monitors and steers the organisational culture to support the direction of the business				DDD PII	SPP LI
Sets the tone for the business by modelling core values			DD	SDP LI	PPI I
Manages expectations about work/life balance				SDD DPP II	PLI

EMPOWERING OTHERS AND BUILDING TEAMS

Behaviour	1	2	3	4	5
Promotes a positive team spirit of mutual respect and support			PP	SDD DLI	P II
Sets clear expectations when delegating			S	DPP II	DDP LI
Adept at judging the appropriate level of challenge for members of the team			PP	SDD DLI I	PI
Builds trust so that team members are comfortable admitting mistakes and can learn from them			S	DDP PLI	DPI I
Able to manage team dynamics			DP	SDP LI	DPI I
Manages conflict in the team openly and constructively			DD	SPP LII I	DP

INVESTOR AND STAKEHOLDER MANAGEMENT

Behaviour	1	2	3	4	5
Cultivates an open, honest relationship with the investor			D	SDP LII	DPP I
Appreciates the risk landscape and the bigger picture from the investor's perspective				DDD PPI I	SPL I
Sets up systems and processes to ensure that the investor receives timely and accurate information			DP	SDP LI	DPI I
Anticipates questions and issues where the investor will require information and explanations			D	DDP PLI II	SP
Draws on support from the investor and promotes a climate of receptiveness to investor involvement in the business			P	SDD DPL II	PI
Ensures decisions and activities are aligned with the investor's long-term plans				DDD PPL III	SP

Judgement

Behaviour	1	2	3	4	5
INSIGHT					
Looks below the surface to identify the root causes of issues			DD	SPP LI	DPI I
Adept at spotting connections and anticipating outcomes				SDD DPP LII	PI
Able to analyse from multiple perspectives			SP	DDD PLI	PII
Quickly able to home in on the most salient issues and establish what is really important			PL	SDD PII	DP
Understands the levers and drivers of value creation and destruction in the business			DP	SDP L	DPI II
Has a balanced understanding of themself and others			DP	DDP LII	SPI
DECISION MAKING					
Confident making decisions across a range of situations, based on whatever time and data are available			P	SDD DPL II	PI
Comfortable taking appropriate risks				DDP PI	SDP LII
Facilitates effective group discussion and decision making			P	SDD PLI I	DPI
Collaborates effectively where possible and appropriate			S	DDD PPLI	PII
Takes full responsibility for own decisions			P	SDD DLI	PPI
Thinks through the consequences of decisions to ensure they are practical			DP	SDP LI	DPI I

Resilience

Behaviour	1	2	3	4	5
DETERMINATION					
Projects a relentless sense of urgency and purpose			DP	DDP LII	SPI
Is driven and goal oriented – persists in the face of obstacles			D	SDP PI	DPL II

(Continued)

Behaviour	1	2	3	4	5
Challenges self and others to make difficult decisions			P	SDD PLI I	DPI
Willing to make short-term sacrifices in the pursuit of longer-term objectives			DP	SDP LII	DPI
Invests time and energy to develop further as a leader			PP	DDL II	SDP I
Effective at dealing with conflict			D	SDP PII	DPL I
WORKING UNDER PRESSURE					
Able to remain calm and clear-thinking under pressure			PP	SDD I	DPL II
Acts as a reassuring presence to others during stressful times				SDD DPP II	PLI
Able to adapt to rapidly changing situations and priorities			P	DDD PLI I	SPI
Sensitive to signs that pressure may be getting to others			P	SDD PI	DPL II
Eliminates unnecessary stress in the business			P	SDD DPL I	PII
Effective at time and work flow management			PP	SDD DI	PLI I

Personal Impact

Behaviour	1	2	3	4	5
STYLE					
Able to engage effectively with people from a wide range of backgrounds and organisational levels			P	SDD DPL II	PI
Projects an appropriate degree of self-confidence and personal conviction			DDP	SDP LII	PI
Shows sensitivity to others' needs and feelings			DP	SDP II	DPL I

Behaviour	1	2	3	4	5
Able to judge the best style with which to challenge others			DP	SDD PLI I	PI
Has effective strategies for influencing upwards and sideways			P	DDP LI	SDP II
Is an effective negotiator				SDD DPP LII	PI
COMMUNICATION Communications are clear and succinct			DP	SDP LII I	DP
Able to adapt mode and style of communication to fit the situation and audience				SDD DPP II	PLI
Actively encourages input from others			DP	SDD PLI I	PI
Listens carefully to check own understanding			D	SDD PPL II	PI
Communicates in good time to ensure 'surprises' are minimised				SDD DPP LII	PI
Can confidently communicate business vision and strategy to a range of audiences				SDD DPP LII	PI

COMPETENCIES IN RANK ORDER

This section shows all of the competencies you requested feedback on, arranged in order of the average of others' ratings. The results do not include your own ratings and are 'weighted' to account for multiple raters of one type, e.g. direct reports, having a disproportionate effect on the overall average rating as compared to a single rater of one type, e.g. manager. The average rating for each type of rater, e.g. direct reports, colleagues, customers, etc. is first produced and then they are used to produce an overall average rating for a competency. This ensures that single (but important) raters like managers get equal weighting in the overall result, giving you a more accurate reflection of how all others rank your competencies.

The chart shows how many ratings the average was derived from (N), the maximum and minimum ratings, and the average rating.

Competency	N	Minimum	Maximum	All others
Setting direction	60	3.0	5.0	4.40
Quality	60	3.0	5.0	4.36
Working under pressure	60	3.0	5.0	4.32
Decision making	60	3.0	5.0	4.24
Determination	60	3.0	5.0	4.21
Empowering others and building teams	60	3.0	5.0	4.19
Investor and stakeholder management	60	3.0	5.0	4.17
Communication	60	3.0	5.0	4.14
Style	60	3.0	5.0	4.12
Insight	60	3.0	5.0	4.11
Goal orientation	60	3.0	5.0	4.06

BEHAVIOURS IN RANK ORDER

This section shows all of the behaviours you requested feedback on, arranged in order of the average of others' ratings. The results do not include your own ratings and are 'weighted' to account for multiple raters of one type, e.g. direct reports, having a disproportionate effect on the overall average rating as compared to a single rater of one type, e.g. manager. The average rating for each type of rater, e.g. direct reports, colleagues, customers, etc. is first produced and then they are used to produce an overall average rating for a behaviour. This ensures that single (but important) raters like managers get equal weighting in the overall result, giving you a more accurate reflection of how all others rank your behaviours. Your raters may have commented on these behaviours in the next section.

The chart shows how many ratings the average was derived from (N), the maximum and minimum ratings, and the average rating.

Behaviour	N	Minimum	Maximum	All others
Conveys a sense of purpose and mission that enthuses others	10	3.0	5.0	4.58
Sets clear expectations when delegating	10	4.0	5.0	4.58
Comfortable taking appropriate risks	10	4.0	5.0	4.58
Strives to share best practice across the business	10	4.0	5.0	4.50
Sensitive to signs that pressure may be getting to others	10	3.0	5.0	4.50
Monitors and steers the organisational culture to support the direction of the business	10	4.0	5.0	4.50
Is driven and goal oriented – persists in the face of obstacles	10	3.0	5.0	4.50
Sets high performance standards for self and others	10	4.0	5.0	4.42
Able to remain calm and clear thinking under pressure	10	3.0	5.0	4.42
Manages expectations about work/life balance	10	4.0	5.0	4.42
Ensures that everyone is driven and focused	10	4.0	5.0	4.42
Effective at dealing with conflict	10	3.0	5.0	4.42
Appreciates the risk landscape and the bigger picture from the investor's perspective	10	4.0	5.0	4.42
Acts as a reassuring presence to others during stressful times	10	4.0	5.0	4.42
Able to adapt mode and style of communication to fit the situation and audience	10	4.0	5.0	4.42
Invests time to understand and exceed customer expectations	10	3.0	5.0	4.33
Effective at time and work flow management	10	3.0	5.0	4.33
Willing to do whatever it takes to deliver at the highest possible standards	10	3.0	5.0	4.33
Shows sensitivity to others' needs and feelings	10	3.0	5.0	4.33
Shares a clear and compelling vision for the future of the business	10	3.0	5.0	4.33
Establishes processes and procedures for managing quality	10	3.0	5.0	4.33

(Continued)

Behaviour	N	Minimum	Maximum	All others
Builds trust so that team members are comfortable admitting mistakes and can learn from them	10	4.0	5.0	4.33
Understands the levers and drivers of value creation and destruction in the business	10	3.0	5.0	4.25
Thinks strategically to develop new products and services which are driven by, and aligned with, future customer needs	10	3.0	5.0	4.25
Has effective strategies for influencing upwards and sideways	10	3.0	5.0	4.25
Cultivates an open, honest relationship with the investor	10	3.0	5.0	4.25
Collaborates effectively where possible and appropriate	10	4.0	5.0	4.25
Able to sustain a high level of productivity whilst maintaining quality	10	3.0	5.0	4.25
Thinks through the consequences of decisions to ensure they are practical	10	3.0	5.0	4.17
Sets up systems and processes to ensure that the investor receives timely and accurate information	10	3.0	5.0	4.17
Sets the tone for the business by modelling core values	10	3.0	5.0	4.17
Eliminates unnecessary stress in the business	10	3.0	5.0	4.17
Able to manage team dynamics	10	3.0	5.0	4.17
Able to analyse from multiple perspectives	10	3.0	5.0	4.17
Takes full responsibility for own decisions	10	3.0	5.0	4.17
Looks below the surface to identify the root causes of issues	10	3.0	5.0	4.17
Is an effective negotiator	10	4.0	5.0	4.17
Facilitates effective group discussion and decision-making	10	3.0	5.0	4.17
Communicates in good time to ensure 'surprises' are minimised	10	4.0	5.0	4.17
Challenges self and others to make difficult decisions	10	3.0	5.0	4.17

Behaviour	N	Minimum	Maximum	All others
Can confidently communicate business vision and strategy to a range of audiences	10	4.0	5.0	4.17
Adept at spotting connections and anticipating outcomes	10	4.0	5.0	4.17
Promotes a positive team spirit of mutual respect and support	10	3.0	5.0	4.08
Willing to make short-term sacrifices in the pursuit of longer-term objectives	10	3.0	5.0	4.08
Listens carefully to check own understanding	10	3.0	5.0	4.08
Invests time and energy to develop further as a leader	10	3.0	5.0	4.08
Initiates changes to organisational structure, systems and processes which match strategic objectives	10	3.0	5.0	4.08
Ensures decisions and activities are aligned with the investor's long-term plans	10	4.0	5.0	4.08
Draws on support from the investor and promotes a climate of receptiveness to investor involvement in the business	10	3.0	5.0	4.08
Confident making decisions across a range of situations, based on whatever time and data are available	10	3.0	5.0	4.08
Allocates resources and effort according to strategic priorities	10	3.0	5.0	4.08
Able to engage effectively with people from a wide range of backgrounds and organisational levels	10	3.0	5.0	4.08
Able to adapt to rapidly changing situations and priorities	10	3.0	5.0	4.08
Sticks with issues until they are properly resolved	10	3.0	5.0	4.00
Communications are clear and succinct	10	3.0	5.0	4.00
Adept at judging the appropriate level of challenge for members of the team	10	3.0	5.0	4.00
Projects a relentless sense of urgency and purpose	10	3.0	5.0	4.00
Monitors progress to ensure delivery	10	3.0	5.0	4.00
Manages conflict in the team openly and constructively	10	3.0	5.0	4.00
Has a balanced understanding of themself and others	10	3.0	5.0	4.00

(Continued)

Behaviour	N	Minimum	Maximum	All others
Anticipates questions and issues, where the investor will require information and explanations	10	3.0	5.0	4.00
Actively encourages input from others	10	3.0	5.0	4.00
Able to judge the best style with which to challenge others	10	3.0	5.0	4.00
Shows absolute commitment to the achievement of business goals	10	3.0	5.0	3.92
Projects an appropriate degree of self-confidence and personal conviction	10	3.0	5.0	3.92
Quickly able to home in on the most salient issues and establish what is really important	10	3.0	5.0	3.92

SCATTERCHART

This report gives you a picture of the overall gap analysis information for each competency. The small unsealed scatterchart shows the actual scores and the main chart is scaled to draw attention to the relative difference between ratings.

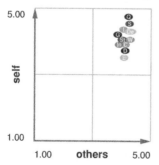

Where there is agreement between the overall ratings that you have given to yourselves with the ratings used by others, then the coordinates will fall either into the top right or bottom left quadrants. You may want to consider how to continue to develop your *confirmed strengths* and make a development plan to meet your *development needs*. The two remaining quadrants invite you to seek more feedback for your comparative *blind spots* and consider how to use your *unrecognised strengths*. Where there is a circle representing a competency on both scatstercharts, then that is the coordinate showing you where your own ratings and those of your respondents have placed you.

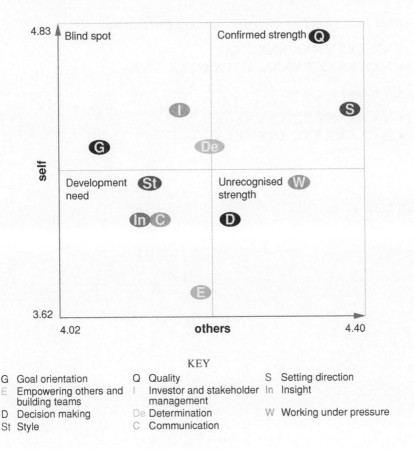

KEY

G	Goal orientation	Q	Quality	S	Setting direction
E	Empowering others and building teams	I	Investor and stakeholder management	In	Insight
D	Decision making	De	Determination	W	Working under pressure
St	Style	C	Communication		

COMMENTS

This section shows the comments your respondents have made. The text of the comments is reproduced here exactly as entered in the questionnaire.

All others

What would you like to see this person STOP doing?

- XXXXXXXXXXXX
- XXXXXXXXXXX

What would you like this person to CONTINUE doing?

• XXXXXXXXXXX

What would you like to see this person START doing?

• XX XXXX XXX XXXX XX
• XXX XXXXX XXXX XXX XXX XX X XX

Any further comments?

• XX XXXXX XX XXX XX
• XX XXX XXXX XXXX XXXX X

Appendix IV

Sample Team Leadership Risk Summary Map

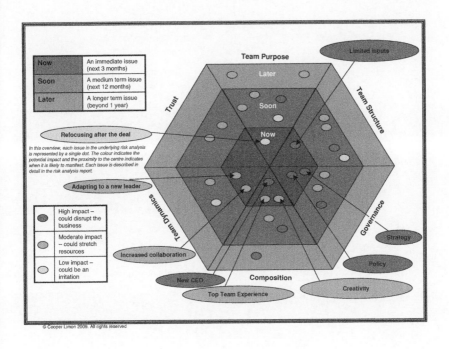

Appendix V

Sample Team Effectiveness Questionnaire

Please use the scale on the right to evaluate the team's effectiveness on each of the following dimensions.

	Strongly disagree	Disagree	Neither agree nor disagree	Agree	Strongly agree
Team purpose					
• A team has a shared view of the overall purpose of the business					
• All members of the team share a single vision of where the business is heading					
• Team members agree on what differentiates the business from the competition					
• The team has specified a set of core values which guide actions within the business					
Team structure					
• The team organises itself effectively to meet the needs of the business					
• Key processes are clear to all members of the team					
• The team has all the data it needs to make decisions					
• The team is able to make decisions as effectively as possible with whatever time and data are available					
• The team has all the information it needs to monitor its own effectiveness					
Governance					
The team understands and spends sufficient time in each of the following areas of governance:					
• Policy formation					
• Clarifying the overall purpose and vision of the business					
• Strategic thinking – looking at where value is added and setting direction					
• Supervising and managing – overseeing the performance of the business					
• Accountability – balancing our responsibility to different stakeholders (employees, customers, suppliers, shareholders, etc.)					

	Strongly disagree	Disagree	Neither agree nor disagree	Agree	Strongly agree
Team composition					
• The collective skills and experience of team members match the needs of the business					
• Individual team members compliment one another because they have a sufficiently wide range of perspectives and outlooks					
• The team has a sufficiently broad repertoire of thinking styles					
• Team members are willing to engage in discussions which are outside of their core area					
• The team is able to adapt its competition in order to match the evolving needs the business as it grows					
Team dynamics					
• Team members feel that participation in the team energises them					
• The team is able to discuss all important issues openly and constructively – even difficult ones					
• The team is able to resolve disagreements quickly and effectively					
• There is a balanced contribution from all members of the team					
• There is a high level of trust and respect among team members					
• Team members hold one another to account and are confident that everyone will do what they say they will					

Appendix VI
Sample Team Dynamics
Summary Map

In this overview, each member of the team is represented by a point around the circle and their scores (from low to high) are represented by distance from the middle

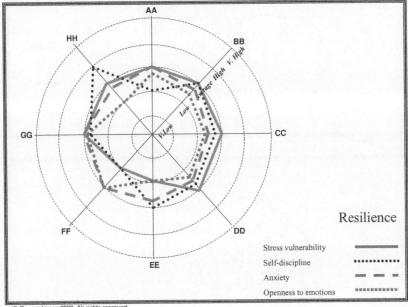

Resilience

Stress vulnerability	————
Self-discipline	••••••••••
Anxiety	— — —
Openness to emotions	▪▪▪▪▪▪▪▪▪

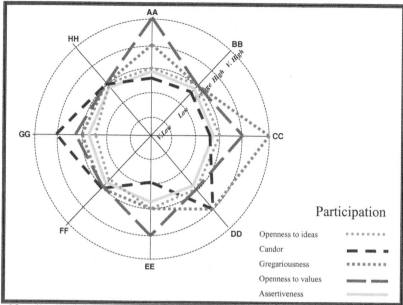

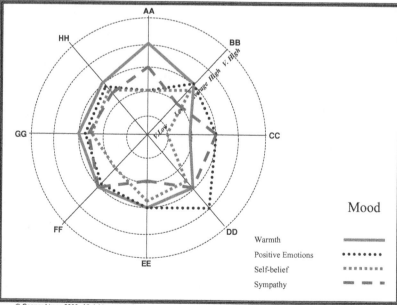

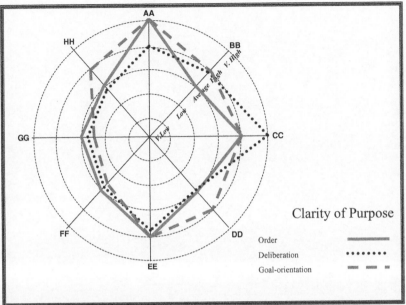

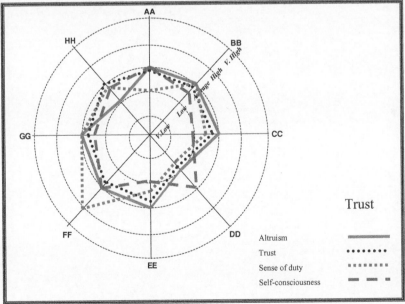

Appendix VII

Sample Aggregate Team Competency Summary[1]

Summary for the board of XYZ Ltd.

This report represents the aggregate feedback responses relating to members of the board of directors of XYZ Ltd as part of the leadership risk-mapping assessment. The purpose of the report is to provide insights into the overall effectiveness of the board, as evaluated by different stakeholder groups, which can be used to inform their approach in leading of XYZ Ltd.

---

[1] Report format reproduced with the kind permission of compass 360.

RESPONSE RANGE_____

RESPONSE RANGE TABLE

This is simply a table showing how people have used the rating scale for each of the questionnaire statements.

You can use this information to identify where you may be coming across differently to different colleagues or groups of colleagues.

In the following table, the distribution of responses from raters is displayed as shaded circles. The size of the circle represents the proportion of raters that gave a particular rating, rather than how many gave that rating.

For example, an average rating of 2, say, in one of the bar charts could have been awarded because everybody agreed to rate you as a 2. But it may be that one person has rated you as a 5, and 3 others have given you a 1. The average is the same, but that average can hide the polarisation of perceptions. It may be useful for you to consider why it is that different people have different opinions of your behaviour.

DELIVERY

Proportion of Respondents

>90%		50%		<5%
●	●	●	●	·

Behaviour		1	2	3	4	5
GOAL ORIENTATION						
Allocates resources and effort according to strategic priorities	subjects				1 ●	2 ●
	direct reports			8 ●		
	peers	1 ·		6 ●	2 ●	
	line managers			3 ●		
	investors				4 ●	2 ●
Initiates changes to organisational structure, systems and processes which match strategic objectives	subjects			3 ●		
	direct reports	1 ·		7 ●		
	peers	1 ·		6 ●	2 ●	
	line managers			3 ●		
	investors				4 ●	2 ●
Thinks strategically to develop new products and services which are driven by, and aligned with, future customer needs	subjects		1 ●			2 ●
	direct reports				7 ●	1 ·
	peers			3 ●	3 ●	3 ●
	line managers				1 ●	2 ●
	investors				5 ●	1 ●

COOPER LIMON LEADERSHIP RISK MAPPING FRAMEWORK©
RESPONSE RANGE_____

Proportion of Respondents

>90%		50%		<5%
●	●	●	●	·

Behaviour		1	2	3	4	5
Shows absolute commitment to the achievement of business goals	subjects				3	
	direct reports			4	2	2
	peers			1	6	2
	line managers				3	
	investors			1	3	2
Monitors progress to ensure delivery	subjects			1	2	
	direct reports			2	6	
	peers			1	5	3
	line managers				2	1
	investors				4	2
Sticks with issues until they are properly resolved	subjects				3	
	direct reports		1	1	4	2
	peers			1	5	3
	line managers			1	1	1
	investors				1	5

QUALITY

Behaviour		1	2	3	4	5
Sets high performance standards for self and others	subjects			2	1	
	direct reports		1	2	5	
	peers				4	5
	line managers				2	1
	investors				3	3
Able to sustain a high level of productivity whilst maintaining quality	subjects			1	1	1
	direct reports		1		4	3
	peers			1	6	2
	line managers				1	2
	investors				1	5
Willing to do whatever it takes to deliver at the highest possible standards	subjects			1	1	1
	direct reports			2	3	3
	peers			1	4	4
	line managers				2	1
	investors				3	3

			Proportion of Respondents			
			>90%	50%		<5%
Behaviour		1	2	3	4	5
Establishes processes and procedures for managing quality	subjects			1		2
	direct reports			1	5	2
	peers			1	6	2
	line managers				2	1
	investors					6
Invests time to understand and exceed customer expectations	subjects				1	2
	direct reports			1	3	4
	peers			2	4	3
	line managers				3	
	investors				2	4
Strives to share best practice across the business	subjects				1	2
	direct reports			1	4	3
	peers				7	2
	line managers				2	1
	investors				4	2

LEADERSHIP

Proportion of Respondents

>90%	50%			<5%
●	●	●	●	·

Behaviour		1	2	3	4	5
SETTING DIRECTION						
Shares a clear and compelling vision for the future of the business	subjects				2	1
	direct reports			2	2	4
	peers			2	3	4
	line managers				2	1
	investors			2	3	1
Ensures that everyone is driven and focused	subjects				2	1
	direct reports			2	3	3
	peers				6	3
	line managers				2	1
	investors			1	3	2
Conveys a sense of purpose and mission that enthuses others	subjects				3	
	direct reports		1	2	2	3
	peers			1	4	4
	line managers				2	1
	investors				3	3
Monitors and steers the organisational culture to support the direction of the business	subjects			1	1	1
	direct reports			1	1	6
	peers				5	4
	line managers				1	2
	investors			1	3	2
Sets the tone for the business by modelling core values	subjects			1	2	
	direct reports			4	2	2
	peers				4	5
	line managers			1	2	
	investors				3	3
Manages expectations about work/life balance	subjects			1	2	
	direct reports			1	6	1
	peers				7	2
	line managers				2	1
	investors				4	2

Proportion of Respondents

>90%	50%	<5%
● ●	●	● ·

Behaviour		1	2	3	4	5
EMPOWERING OTHERS AND BUILDING TEAMS						
Promotes a positive team spirit of mutual respect and support	subjects			1 ●	2 ●	
	direct reports			2 ●	3 ●	3 ●
	peers			2	3	4
	line managers			1 ●	2 ●	
	investors				3	3
Sets clear expectations when delegating	subjects			2 ●	1 ●	
	direct reports				4 ●	4 ●
	peers			6	3	
	line managers				2 ●	1 ●
	investors				5	1
Adept at judging the appropriate level of challenge for members of the team	subjects			1 ●	2 ●	
	direct reports			2 ●	4 ●	2 ●
	peers			2	3	4
	line managers				3	
	investors				4	2
Builds trust so that team members are comfortable admitting mistakes and can learn from them	subjects			1 ●	2 ●	
	direct reports			3 ●	2 ●	3 ●
	peers				5	4
	line managers				2 ●	1 ●
	investors				4	2
Able to manage team dynamics	subjects			1 ●	1 ●	1 ●
	direct reports			4 ●	1 ·	3 ●
	peers			1	4	4
	line managers				2 ●	1 ●
	investors				3	3
Manages conflict in the team openly and constructively	subjects				3 ●	
	direct reports			5 ●	1 ·	2 ●
	peers				7	2
	line managers				2 ●	1 ●
	investors			1	4	1

Proportion of Respondents

	>90%	50%	<5%
	● ●	●	● ·

Behaviour		1	2	3	4	5
INVESTOR AND STAKEHOLDER MANAGEMENT						
Cultivates an open, honest relationship with the investor	subjects				2	1
	direct reports			2	5	1
	peers			1	4	4
	line managers				2	1
	investors				5	1
Appreciates the risk landscape and the bigger picture from the investor's perspective	subjects				2	1
	direct reports			1	5	2
	peers			1	4	4
	line managers				1	2
	investors			1	4	1
Sets up systems and processes to ensure that the investor receives timely and accurate information	subjects			1	2	
	direct reports			2	3	3
	peers			2	3	4
	line managers			3		
	investors			4	2	
Anticipates questions and issues, where the investor will require information and explanations	subjects				2	1
	direct reports			2	4	2
	peers				5	4
	line managers				2	1
	investors			6		
Draws on support from the investor and promotes a climate of receptiveness to investor involvement in the business	subjects			3		
	direct reports			2	4	2
	peers			1	4	4
	line managers			3		
	investors			4	2	
Ensures decisions and activities are aligned with the investor's long-term plans	subjects				2	1
	direct reports			2	5	1
	peers			6	3	
	line managers			3		
	investors			6		

JUDGEMENT

Proportion of Respondents

>90%	50%	<5%		
●	●	●	●	·

Behaviour		1	2	3	4	5
INSIGHT						
Looks below the surface to identify the root causes of issues	subjects				3 ●	
	direct reports		2 ●	2 ●	2 ●	2 ●
	peers				6 ●	3 ●
	line managers			1 ●	2 ●	
	investors				4 ●	2 ●
Adept at spotting connections and anticipating outcomes	subjects				3 ●	
	direct reports			2 ●	5 ●	1 ●
	peers			1 ●	3 ●	5 ●
	line managers				3 ●	
	investors				5 ●	1 ●
Able to analyse from multiple perspectives	subjects			1 ●	2 ●	
	direct reports		1 ●	2 ●	4 ●	1 ●
	peers			1 ●	6 ●	2 ●
	line managers			1 ●	2 ●	
	investors				2 ●	4 ●
Quickly able to home in on the most salient issues and establish what is really important	subjects			1 ●	2 ●	
	direct reports		1 ●		4 ●	3 ●
	peers			1 ●	6 ●	2 ●
	line managers			1 ●	2 ●	
	investors				3 ●	3 ●
Understands the levers and drivers of value creation and destruction in the business	subjects				3 ●	
	direct reports		1 ●	3 ●	2 ●	2 ●
	peers			1 ●	6 ●	2 ●
	line managers			1 ●	1 ●	1 ●
	investors				2 ●	4 ●
Has a balanced understanding of themselves and others	subjects				2 ●	1 ●
	direct reports			3 ●	4 ●	1 ●
	peers			1 ●	6 ●	2 ●
	line managers				3 ●	
	investors				4 ●	2 ●

Proportion of Respondents

	>90%	50%	<5%
●	● ●	●	·

Behaviour		1	2	3	4	5
DECISION MAKING						
Confident making decisions across a range of situations, based on whatever time and data are available	subjects				3	
	direct reports			3	4	1
	peers			1	4	4
	line managers				3	
	investors				4	2
Comfortable taking appropriate risks	subjects				2	1
	direct reports			2	3	3
	peers			1	5	3
	line managers				2	1
	investors				2	4
Facilitates effective group discussion and decision-making	subjects				3	
	direct reports			2	4	2
	peers			1	5	3
	line managers				2	1
	investors				3	3
Collaborates effectively where possible and appropriate	subjects			1	2	
	direct reports			2	4	2
	peers			1	5	3
	line managers				3	
	investors				1	5
Takes full responsibility for own decisions	subjects			1	1	1
	direct reports			1	7	
	peers			1	4	4
	line managers				3	
	investors				4	2
Thinks through the consequences of decisions to ensure they are practical	subjects				3	
	direct reports			3	4	1
	peers			1	5	3
	line managers				3	
	investors				2	4

RESILIENCE

Proportion of Respondents

>90%	50%	<5%
●	● ● ● ·	

Behaviour		1	2	3	4	5

DETERMINATION

Behaviour	Respondent	1	2	3	4	5
Projects a relentless sense of urgency and purpose	subjects				1 ●	2 ●
	direct reports			2 ●	5 ●	1 ·
	peers			1 ·	4 ●	4 ●
	line managers				3 ●	
	investors				5 ●	1 ·
Is driven and goal oriented – persists in the face of obstacles	subjects				3 ●	
	direct reports			1 ●	5 ●	2 ●
	peers			1 ·	4 ●	4 ●
	line managers			1 ●		2 ●
	investors				3 ●	3 ●
Challenges self and others to make difficult dicisions	subjects				3 ●	
	direct reports			1 ·	4 ●	3 ●
	peers			1 ●	5 ●	3 ●
	line managers				2 ●	1 ●
	investors				5 ●	1 ·
Willing to make short-term sacrifices in the pursuit of longer-term objectives	subjects				3 ●	
	direct reports			3 ●	2 ●	3 ●
	peers			1 ·	5 ●	3 ●
	line managers				2 ●	1 ●
	investors				5 ●	1 ·
Invests time and energy to develop further as a leader	subjects				2 ●	1 ●
	direct reports			2 ●	3 ●	3 ●
	peers			2 ●	5 ●	2 ●
	line managers				2 ●	1 ●
	investors				5 ●	1 ·
Effective at dealing with conflict	subjects				3 ●	
	direct reports			3 ●	2 ●	3 ●
	peers				5 ●	4 ●
	line managers				2 ●	1 ●
	investors				5 ●	1 ·

Proportion of Respondents

	>90%	50%		<5%
●	●	●	●	·

Behaviour		1	2	3	4	5

WORKING UNDER PRESSURE

Behaviour	Respondents	1	2	3	4	5
Able to remain calm and clear-thinking under pressure	subjects				3	
	direct reports		·	1	4	3
	peers			2	3	4
	line managers				2	1
	investors				4	2
Acts as a reassuring presence to others during stressful times	subjects				3	
	direct reports		1		5	2
	peers				6	3
	line managers				2	1
	investors				4	2
Able to adapt to rapidly changing situations and priorities	subjects			1		2
	direct reports		·	1	5	2
	peers			1	4	4
	line managers			1	2	
	investors				5	1
Sensitive to signs that pressure may be getting to others	subjects				3	
	direct reports			2	3	3
	peers			1	5	3
	line managers				2	1
	investors				4	2
Eliminates unnecessary stress in the business	subjects				3	
	direct reports				6	2
	peers			1	4	4
	line managers				3	
	investors				4	2
Effective at time and work flow management	subjects				3	
	direct reports			2	4	2
	peers			2	3	4
	line managers				2	1
	investors				3	3

PERSONAL IMPACT

	Proportion of Respondents		
	>90%	50%	<5%
	●	● ● ●	·

Behaviour		1	2	3	4	5
STYLE						
Able to engage effectively with people from a wide range of backgrounds and organisational levels	subjects				3	
	direct reports			1	6	1
	peers			1	5	3
	line managers				2	1
	investors				5	1
Projects an appropriate degree of self-confidence and personal conviction	subjects				3	
	direct reports			4	3	1
	peers			1	5	3
	line managers				3	
	investors				4	2
Shows sensitivity to others' needs and feelings	subjects			1	2	
	direct reports			3	2	3
	peers			2	5	2
	line managers				2	1
	investors				5	1
Able to judge the best style with which to challenge others	subjects				2	1
	direct reports			3	4	1
	peers			1	4	4
	line managers				3	
	investors				5	1
Has effective strategies for influencing upwards and sideways	subjects				2	1
	direct reports			1	4	3
	peers			1	5	3
	line managers				3	
	investors				4	2
Is an effective negotiator	subjects				2	1
	direct reports			2	4	2
	peers				6	3
	line managers				2	1
	investors				5	1

Proportion of Respondents

>90%		50%		<5%
●	●	●	●	·

Behaviour		1	2	3	4	5

COMMUNICATION

		1	2	3	4	5
Communications are clear and succinct	subjects			3 ●		
	direct reports		3 ●	2 ●	3 ●	
	peers		1 ·	5 ●	3 ●	
	line managers			3 ●		
	investors			6 ●		
Able to adapt mode and style of communication to fit the situation and audience	subjects			3 ●		
	direct reports		2 ●	4 ●	2 ●	
	peers			5 ●	4 ●	
	line managers		1 ●	1 ●	1 ●	
	investors			4 ●	2 ●	
Actively encourages input from others	subjects		1 ●	2 ●		
	direct reports		1 ·	6 ●	1 ●	
	peers		1 ·	4 ●	4 ●	
	line managers			3 ●		
	investors			4 ●	2 ●	
Listens carefully to check own understanding	subjects			3 ●		
	direct reports		1 ·	6 ●	1 ●	
	peers			5 ●	4 ●	
	line managers			2 ●	1 ●	
	investors			5 ●	1 ●	
Communicates in good time to ensure 'surprises' are minimised	subjects			3 ●		
	direct reports		2 ●	5 ●	1 ●	
	peers			6 ●	3 ●	
	line managers			3 ●		
	investors			5 ●	1 ●	
Can confidently communicate business vision and strategy to a range of audience	subjects			2 ●	1 ●	
	direct reports			6 ●	2 ●	
	peers			6 ●	3 ●	
	line managers			3 ●		
	investors			5 ●	1 ·	

COMPETENCIES IN RANK ORDER_____

This section shows all of the competencies you requested feedback on, arranged in order of the average of others' ratings. The results are 'weighted' to account for multiple raters of one type, e.g direct reports, having a disproportionate effect on the overall average rating as compared to a single rater of one type, e.g manager. The average rating for each type of rater, e.g. direct reports, colleagues, customers, etc. is first produced and then they are used to produce an overall average rating for a competency. This ensures that single (but important) raters like managers get equal weighting in the overall result, giving you a more accurate reflection of how all others rank your competencies. This chart shows how many ratings the average was derived from (N), the maximum and minimum ratings, and the average rating.

Competency	N	minimum	maximum	All others
Quality	156	2.0	5.0	4.37
Working under pressure	156	2.0	5.0	4.23
Decision making	156	3.0	5.0	4.21
Determination	156	3.0	5.0	4.21
Setting direction	156	2.0	5.0	4.20
Empowering others and building teams	156	3.0	5.0	4.20
Investor and stakeholder management	156	3.0	5.0	4.17
Communication	156	3.0	5.0	4.16
Goal orientaion	156	2.0	5.0	4.14
Style	156	3.0	5.0	4.14
Insight	156	2.0	5.0	4.06

Appendix VIII

Sample Organisational
Leadership Risk Summary Map

In this overview, each issue in the underlying risk analysis is represented by a single dot. The colour indicates the potential impact and the proximity to the centre indicates when it is likely to manifest. Each issue is described in detail in the risk analysis report.

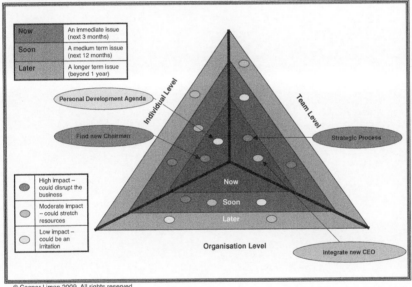

Appendix IX

Sample Cultural Risk Map

Artefacts (tangible expressions of culture such as buildings and designs)

Within the next eighteen months it is likely that the administrative centre of the business will move as part of a planned acquisition. The business has been based in the current building since it was founded in 1974 so it is likely that, for many longer serving employees, there will be a strong association with the current buildings. It is important that the move to the new building is positioned and communicated sensitively and care should be taken to identify indications of cultural resistance.

Risk Evaluation:

Impact:′ ⬤   Low – could be an irritation

Timeframe: Medium term

Structures and behaviours (the way the business is structured and the style of leadership and management)

➢ The current head office has always represented the hub of the business. With the planned expansion of the overseas operations and the acquisition which is planned in year 2, the proportion of revenues attributable to the part of the business located in the UK headquarters will decrease substantially. It is, therefore, important that the focus of the tension and the perspective of the leadership team becomes much more global. The capacity of the senior management population to think globally is untested and it will be important to make time for them to expand and develop their thinking appropriately. As the business develops, management should be alert to signs of cultural resistance to international growth.

Impact: ● Moderate – could stretch resources

Timeframe: Medium term

➢ The prominent leadership style within the business has been 'command and control' as dictated by the two founding Partners who have driven all significant business decisions. Following the buy-out, one of the founding Partners will be retiring and the other will be stepping down and adopting a more advisory role. To achieve the planned growth and the organisational flexibility which this will require, the new leadership team will have to evolve a more collaborative style of leadership. In the first instance, members of the new Board will need to be comfortable in engaging with the significantly increased level of authority and executive control which they now have. In doing this, it will be useful for them to draw on one another's support and develop a broader repertoire of leadership styles and approaches when it comes to making significant business decisions.

Impact: ● Moderate – could stretch resources

Timeframe: Short term

Values (the fundamental shared beliefs about what drives value in the business)

Traditionally, there has been a belief in the business that any borrowing should be kept to an absolute minimum. Significant debt has been seen as something which is 'bad'. For the next few years, borrowing will be inevitable and necessary to drive the planned growth. The leadership team will, therefore, have to revise their beliefs around business debt and cultivate a much greater comfort with the use of borrowed funds to grow the business and the risks which that will bring.

Impact: ●   Moderate – could stretch resources

Time frame: Medium term

Meanings and symbols (private, often unspoken associations made by people within the business)

The two founding Partners have been a dominant influence within the business and for many people at different levels, these two individuals in a way represent the business. As these two will no longer be playing an active role in the day-to-day running of the business, it is to be expected that their departure may provoke a period of 'organisational grieving' at their departure. Whilst an inevitable process, it is important that this does not drain energy or impede growth. As the new Chief Executive integrates into his role, it will be important for him to explore ways in which he can imprint his own personality on the business and build trust and confidence at all levels as quickly as possible.

Impact: ○   Low – could be an irritation

Time frame: Short term

Unconscious assumptions (unconscious thoughts about the business which drive behaviour)

Assumptions about each of the following areas may or will be challenged within the context of the new strategy and could, therefore, prompt resistance:

- **Business drivers** – many people have held a belief that the business is driven by the two founding Partners. This belief will have to be adapted to reflect a reality where it is the new Chief Executive together with his Board who drive the business

- **Style of governance** – instead of all key decisions being made by one or both of the founding Partners there will be more group decision-making

- **Time perspective** – traditionally the focus has been rather short term and based around reactive, tactical thinking. Going forward the business will need to think further ahead and be more strategic

- **Margins** – in the past, high costs incurred in the corporate headquarters have been permissible along with some extravagance on the part of the owners of the business. Going forward it will fall to members of the new Board to model the importance of cost awareness

- **Risk appetite** – traditionally the business has been highly risk averse. To achieve the growth foreseen, leaders and managers will need to become more comfortable taking risks and making decisions under conditions of increased uncertainty

Impact: ⬤   Moderate – could stretch resources

Time frame: Short to medium term

Index

Printed and bound by CPI Group (UK) Ltd, Croydon, CR0 4YY